COUNT
THE
WINGS

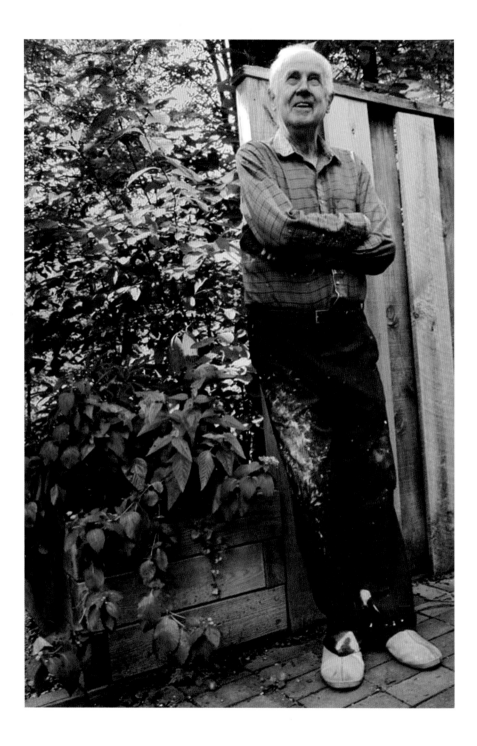

COUNT
THE
WINGS

the life and art of Charley Harper

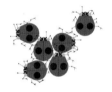

Michelle Houts

BIOGRAPHIES FOR YOUNG READERS

Ohio University Press
Athens

Ohio University Press, Athens, Ohio 45701
ohioswallow.com
© 2018 by Michelle Houts

To obtain permission to quote, reprint, or otherwise reproduce or distribute
material from Ohio University Press publications, please contact our rights
and permissions department at (740) 593-1154 or (740) 593-4536 (fax).

Printed in the United States of America
Ohio University Press books are printed on acid-free paper ∞™

28 27 26 25 24 23 22 21 20 19 18   5 4 3 2 1

Frontispiece: Charley Harper at home in his favorite working pants.
Charley used his right leg to wipe his paintbrushes. *Photo by Todd Oldham*
Cover art: Mystery of the Missing Migrants. Courtesy of Charley Harper Art Studio

Library of Congress Cataloging-in-Publication Data

Names: Houts, Michelle, author.
Title: Count the wings : the life and art of Charley Harper / Michelle Houts.
Description: Athens, Ohio : Ohio University Press, 2018. | Series:
  Biographies for young readers | Includes bibliographical references. |
  Audience: Ages 8-13.
Identifiers: LCCN 2018004881 ISBN 9780821423073 (hardback) | ISBN
  9780821423080 (pb) | ISBN 9780821446355 (pdf)
Subjects: LCSH: Harper, Charley, 1922-2007--Juvenile literature. |
  Artists--United States--Biography--Juvenile literature.
Classification: LCC N6537.H3495 H68 2018 | DDC 700.92 [B] --dc23
LC record available at https://lccn.loc.gov/2018000488

Contents

Author's Note

(As Close as I'll Ever Get to) A Day with Charley Harper

It's midmorning as I wind my way down a narrow lane to the Harper home and studio. It's the very beginning of a journey, and I'm excited and a little bit nervous, too. I had heard of Charley Harper, the artist. I had seen his bold, bright artwork on everything from art gallery walls to T-shirts. I'd prepared for my visit, reading everything I could find about the man. Still, I'm feeling a little uncertain. Am I in the right place? And then it comes into view—the Harper home and studio, tucked away on five acres of wooded terrain in the middle of a midcentury Cincinnati neighborhood. I get out of my car as Charley and Edie Harper's only son, Brett, emerges with a smile and a wave.

The home and studio, built in 1958, are separate structures designed to blend with each other and with the surrounding hillside and beech forest. A boardwalk and overhead wisteria vines create an outdoor corridor between two sets of sliding glass doors. I think about how that two-way path flows between the house and studio—how it connected Charley's family life with his work.

The studio's two current rooms sit in stark contrast to one another. The newer of the two, a 1999 addition, is bright white with modern shelving, framed art, and a large, open work area. Charley's signature red cardinal and ladybug appear prominently here.

When I venture up a single step and through a narrow doorway, I feel as if I've stepped back in time. This, the original 1958 room, was Charley's space and it's filled—floor to ceiling—with books and magazines, file cabinets, and chests of drawers. Allowing just enough room for me to squeeze through, a narrow path leads to the back of the small room, where Charley's desk sits, untouched since his death in 2007. On the desk, the blue and black paints, sketches, and reference books are evidence of Charley's last painting, *Scary Scenario*. The *National Geographic Book of Mammals* lies open, and a swimming polar bear stares up at me as it once stared up at Charley.

Back in the other room, Brett and the Harper Studio's **archivist** and **curator**, Chip Doyle, have arranged family photographs on a table for me to look at and scan into my computer. They've asked for my wish list of the materials I need to begin my research of Charley's life and work. It's almost with embarrassment that I provide such a list, which includes childhood photographs, letters, grade cards, art school documents, wedding pictures, awards, and commendations. Is it too personal, what I'm asking? But Brett doesn't blink an eye.

"Put me in, Coach," Chip says. "What do you need?" I glance up at Brett to see if he's going to answer, but Chip is looking at me. They pull up a stool for me with an old green field jacket hanging over the back and we get to work. Brett and Chip dig through boxes and albums as I scan articles, documents, and photographs.

"Look at this!" and "Now here's something I've never seen!" are two phrases often repeated as they open more boxes and uncover artifacts long forgotten. Charley's possessions, still strewn about the studio as if he had been there yesterday, are treated with a unique combination of respect and practicality. That field jacket on the back of my stool, Chip mentions casually, was Charley's. It's his U.S. Army jacket from World War II, bearing the Timberwolf insignia of the 104th Infantry Division. A treasured possession, it hasn't left the stool for eight years. And yet, if I said I was cold, I'm pretty sure someone would say, "There's a jacket on the back of your stool. Put it on."

Hours pass in a heartbeat. Picture by picture, piece by piece, Charley's life unfolds before my eyes. We've only scratched the surface. There's more to do, more to see, many more questions to ask. But the artist who was a mystery to me is now a real person. His passions and dreams are becoming clearer; his story is beginning to form in my head.

The fact that Charley is becoming more real to me is both a relief and a terrifying realization. As I pack up my work, say goodbye until next time, and get into my car, my head swims with doubts. Will I be able to do this man justice in telling his story? How do I capture the essence of this gentle soul, so in tune with nature and with people? Will I be able to connect today's youth with this artist whose work they've likely seen but whose name they may not know?

I maneuver my car around on the only flat ground on the rolling property, then point it out the long, wooded lane toward the surrounding neighborhood. It's late afternoon, and the sun hasn't made much of an appearance all day. The October landscape is brightened by the yellow and gold leaves that defy the wind and refuse to fall. November is just around the corner.

The driveway is so narrow that small branches brush my car as I pass. I round the bend, still feeling the weight of my own doubt. My eyes shift suddenly to the left. *A flash of red. A dip and dart.* And he's gone. He had been swift, for sure, but he'd lingered just long enough to let me know he was there. *A cardinal.* I smile, then laugh out loud.

Charley Harper's cardinal.

All my misgivings fade with the sound of my own laughter. I'm ready to do this. I'm ready to tell you about Charley Harper, the artist.

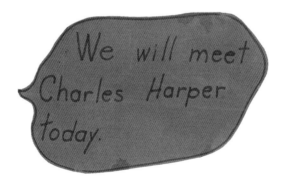

Charley placed this sign, a memento from a visit to a local elementary school, on his studio door.
Photo by the author

COUNT
THE
WINGS

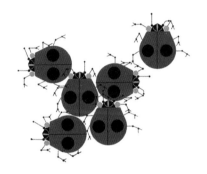

1

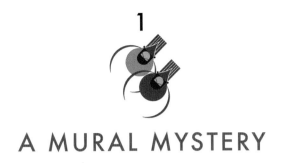

A MURAL MYSTERY

I asked one of the guys who had done construction with the
city if there were some murals covered up and he said, "Yes.
You've got two murals in there."

—Ric Booth, General Manager,
Duke Energy Convention Center[1]

O N A MONDAY afternoon in August 2014, a small group of people
gathered inside the Duke Energy Convention Center in downtown Cincinnati, Ohio. Among them were a city council member, a
newspaper reporter, and some folks who worked for the convention
center. They stood in front of a small hole that had been recently cut in
the wall. One by one, while a maintenance worker held a flashlight to
illuminate the darkness, the people peered inside.

What had everyone so intrigued?

Behind the wall stood a very large **mosaic** mural designed by one
of Cincinnati's favorite artists, Charles Burton Harper. A person wouldn't
have to spend much time in Cincinnati to know just how much the
city loves Charley Harper's work. In fact, a few blocks from the convention center is a six-story building bearing Charley's painting
Homecoming, in which a bluebird pair inspects a potential home for
their brood. This larger-than-life project was funded by Cincinnati's

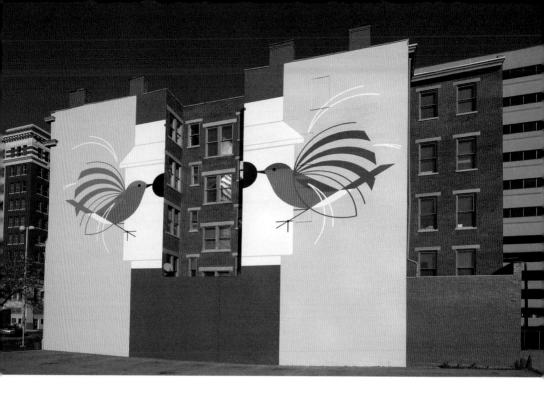

HOMECOMING

Homecoming (Bluebirds) © 2012 ArtWorks / Charley Harper/119 East Court Street, Cincinnati, OH/photo by J. Miles Wolf

ArtWorks and painted by artist Jenny Ustick, two art teachers, and twelve students.

Atop one of the city's seven hills, another ArtWorks project, the Cincinnati Zoo's City Barn, bears many of Harper's designs. Even visitors to the John Weld Peck Federal Building, located downtown, find themselves surrounded by Charley's *Space for All Species* tile mural as they wait for an elevator.

Why, then, if Charley Harper's work is so revered, would a mural —actually two murals—be hidden away beneath the walls of the convention center? Who covered them and why? And now that there's a hole in the wall through which the colorful tiles can be viewed, will the murals see daylight once more?

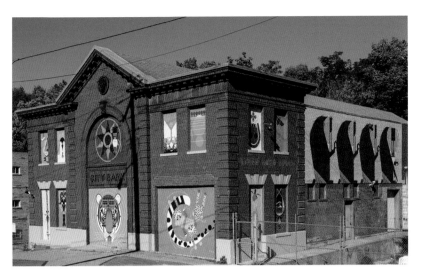

THE ZOO BARN

Charley Harper's Beguiled by the Wild © 2014 ArtWorks/Charley Harper/3512 Vine Street, Cincinnati, OH/photo by J. Miles Wolf

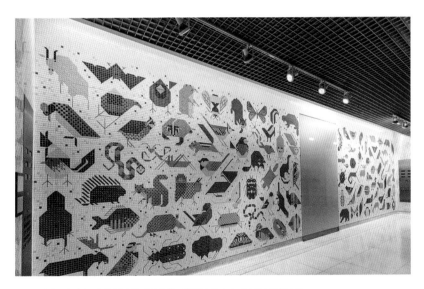

THE MURAL AT THE PECK FEDERAL BUILDING

Courtesy of Charley Harper Art Studio. Photo by Ross Van Pelt-RVP Photography

To discover the answers to these questions, we'll have to find out more about Charley Harper, the artist. So, let's start where Charley started—on a farm in West Virginia.

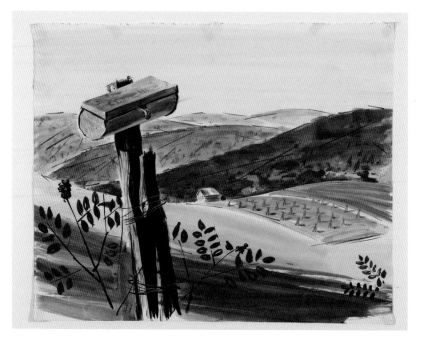

HARPER FARM WITH MAILBOX

Even though farming wasn't in his future, Charley connected with the West Virginia countryside he called home for the first nineteen years of his life.

Courtesy of Charley Harper Art Studio

2

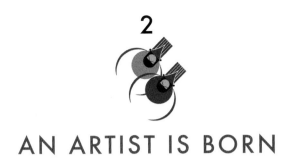

AN ARTIST IS BORN

Every time I hear the trains, I'm transported back to the farm.

—Charley Harper[1]

A YOUNG CHARLEY HARPER lay mesmerized on the creek bank, well aware that he should be headed home. There were, after all, plenty of chores to do on his family's farm near Frenchton, West Virginia. It wouldn't be fair if his older sisters Ruth and Reta (nicknamed Reed) had to hoe the corn, feed the chickens, bale the hay, and milk the cows without him. But Charley stayed near the water. He couldn't tear himself away from what was happening right before his eyes.

There, on the surface of the still water, bugs were gliding. The water striders were long-legged critters whose miniscule feet barely skimmed the water. "Jesus bugs" Charley had heard them called. He'd been to Sunday School where he'd heard that Jesus—just like these graceful bugs—had walked on water. Their balancing act would have been enough to impress any observant young boy, but Charley had noticed something more: shadows. The sun's rays filtered through the shallow water and the bugs' narrow bodies left shadows on the creekbed. Add fascinating circles where the bugs' feet touched the surface, and the result was something Charley could have examined for hours.

Many years later, Charley would recreate those lines and circles in a painting he called *Jesus Bugs.*

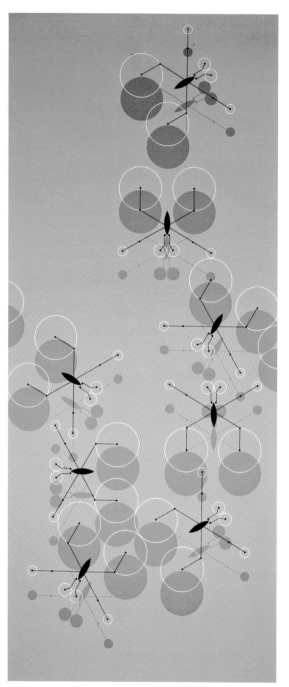

JESUS BUGS

When asked if he had a favorite painting, Charley always answered *Jesus Bugs*. His earliest memories of these surface-skating insects are also his earliest memories of connecting with nature.

Courtesy of Charley Harper Art Studio. Photo by Ross Van Pelt-RVP Photography

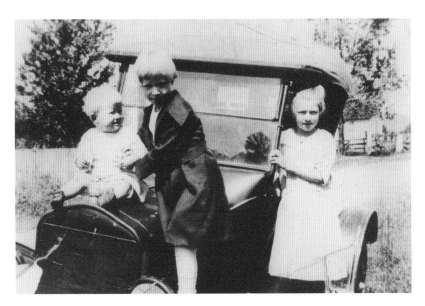

Baby Charley with his two older sisters, Ruth and Reta.
Courtesy of Charley Harper Art Studio

Charley didn't like farming very much, and he knew that from a very young age.[2] Despite this, he always looked back on his childhood in Upshur County, West Virginia, with fond memories. As a boy, Charley attended reunions and Sunday church services with his family. The Harpers made trips to town in an old Ford Model T car. The children went sledding in the winter. In the springtime, while roaming the hills near his home, Charley learned to appreciate the trilling sound of **spring peepers**. The song of the small chorus frog would always remind him of home.

When Charley's family sold the farm and moved into the small town of French Creek, Charley's father ran a feed store, above which the family lived. French Creek itself ran right through town, and Charley spent a great deal of time fishing there, using crayfish from the creek as bait.

Charley attended a three-room schoolhouse where, when he was in the fourth grade, he discovered that he could draw better than anyone else in his class. It was the only thing he could do better than his

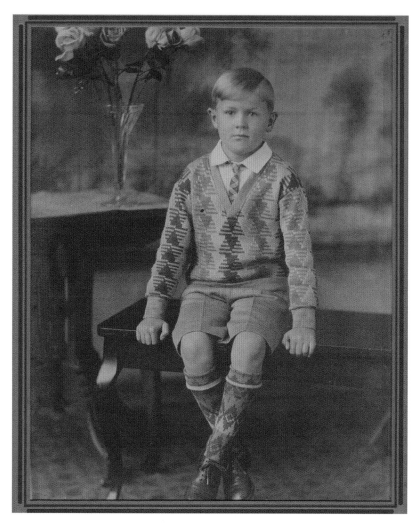

Charley's grade-school report card contained marks for reading, writing,
spelling, arithmetic, geography, and hygiene. The line for "Drawing"
remained blank all year, as art was not taught in his school.
Courtesy of Charley Harper Art Studio

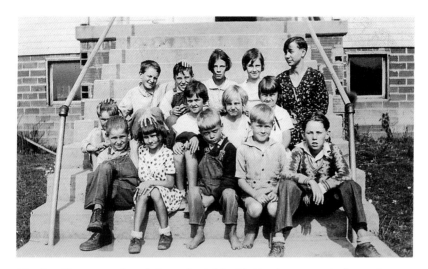

Charley *(front row, fourth from the left)* with his classmates in front of Frenchton School in West Virginia.
Courtesy of Charley Harper Art Studio

peers, he said. He was a good student, but he quickly figured out that he could get even better grades in both English and history if he added a few illustrations to his homework papers. Charley liked to tell the story of how he once saved his history grade by drawing all the presidents.

Charley attended Buckhannon-Upshur High School, nine miles north of French Creek. There his fondness for art and his confusion regarding his future grew. He knew he didn't want to be a farmer or run his father's feed store, but no one he knew had actually made a living as an artist.[3] As not a single art class was offered in school, Charley enrolled in a **correspondence course** in cartooning. Assignments were mailed to him, and he'd send back his work for evaluation.

Charley must have enjoyed learning to draw cartoons. He put his skills to good use, sketching all of his classmates—including two who refused to pose.

By the time he graduated from high school in 1939, Charley had decided that it didn't matter if he was the only artist he knew. He was going to choose art as a career.

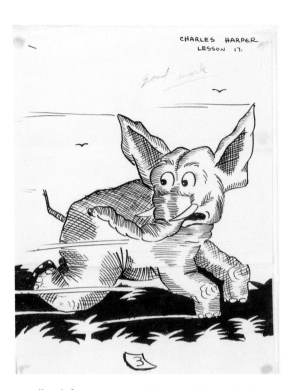

Feedback from Charley's correspondence school instructor says, "Good work," and, "Legs are too long for donkey." Courtesy of Charley Harper Art Studio. Photo by Ross Van Pelt-RVP Photography

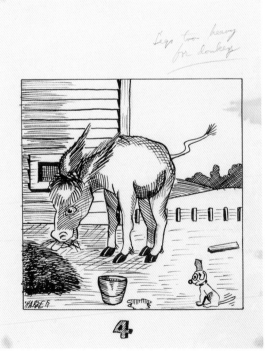

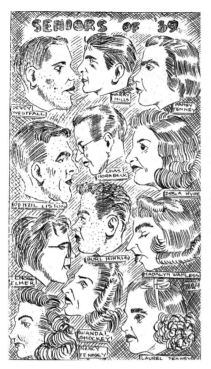

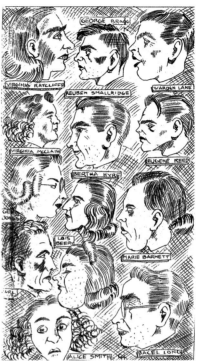

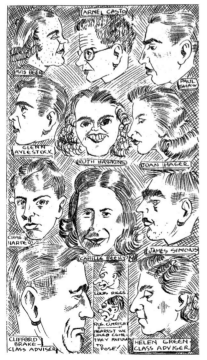

Charley put his cartooning skills to good use with these caricatures of each member of the Buckhannon-Upshur High School Class of 1939.

Images courtesy of the Upshur County Historical Society, Buckhannon, West Virginia

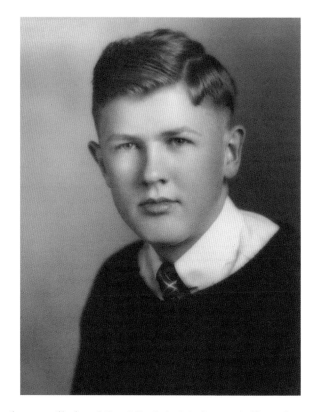

In 1939, Charley graduated from Buckhannon-Upshur High School, which he affectionately called "Buck-Up High."
Courtesy of Charley Harper Art Studio

That fall, Charley enrolled at West Virginia Wesleyan College, located in Buckhannon. He was pleased to find that art classes were offered, but disappointed when he realized that most of his time would be spent copying calendar pictures.[4] He had hoped he would learn the basics of drawing and study the masters of fine art. Once, Charley left a diary he was required to keep for his freshman English class in the art room. His art instructor, Lita Snodgrass, found it and read that Charley didn't think she was a very good teacher and that he felt he likely knew more about art than she did. If Ms. Snodgrass had taken offense at his comments, Charley's art career may have ended right then and there. But she had seen Charley's talent and, in Charley's words, she "forgave me very gallantly."[5] It was Lita Snodgrass who first suggested Charley consider attending the Art Academy of Cincinnati, a well-regarded institution 300 miles to the west.

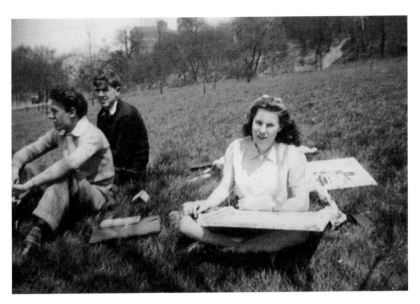

Charley *(center)* and Edie *(right)* spent many hours sketching and painting together while attending the Art Academy of Cincinnati.
Courtesy of Charley Harper Art Studio

To a West Virginia farm boy, the big city of Cincinnati, Ohio, seemed quite far from home. To his parents, it must have seemed even farther. Though he had great respect for the people of French Creek and Buckhannon, Charley felt that no one there truly understood his life's goals. His father, certainly, couldn't imagine why his son would want to leave the small town, and his mother cried when he left by train in September 1940.[6]

It didn't take long for Charley to find someone who did understand him. On his first day of class at the Art Academy of Cincinnati, he made a friend. Her name was Edith McKee, and she was an only child whose family lived in Roselawn, a Cincinnati suburb. Charley soon became a frequent dinner guest at the McKee house. He enjoyed the home-cooked meals, and Mr. and Mrs. McKee seemed to understand Charley's desire to be an artist in a way his own mother and father hadn't. Perhaps it was because their own daughter, whom everyone called Edie, shared similar ambitions. Eventually, Edie made the trip to West Virginia

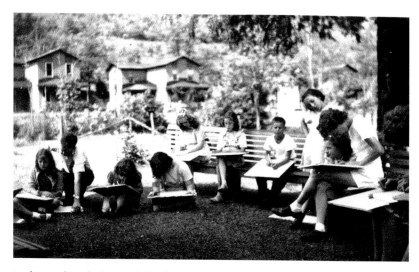

In this undated photo, likely from the early 1940s, Charley *(second from left)* is seen teaching a drawing lesson to a group of 4-H campers near Selbyville, West Virginia.
Courtesy of Charley Harper Art Studio

to meet Charley's family, where she was received enthusiastically by the Harpers. She especially enjoyed the company of Charley's sisters.

Art school in Cincinnati was everything Charley had hoped it would be. He learned the basics of drawing and how to paint realistically. He studied sculpture, airbrush technique, printmaking, and **serigraphy**, or silkscreening. Charley absorbed each new class with great enthusiasm. He knew he was in the right place. Of course, it didn't hurt that his new friend Edie was in nearly every class he took.

After a year at the Art Academy of Cincinnati, Charley returned home for the summer break. Back in West Virginia, he took a job bagging groceries and sweeping up at the local A&P grocery store. It wasn't long before his employer recognized Charley's talented hand. Soon Charley was lettering all the signs in the store.

When he wasn't working, Charley was fishing or drawing. On the first day of fishing season, he was so eager to get started, he and a friend went fishing near the church while Sunday School was in session, which,

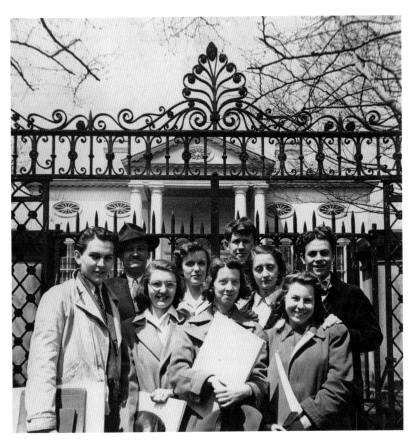

Charley *(back row, center)* and Edie *(front, right)* on a field trip to the Taft Museum with Art Academy classmates.
Courtesy of Charley Harper Art Studio

according to Charley, "in French Creek, constitutes a near-scandal." He told Edie later, "I did have a guilty conscience, didn't catch any."[7]

Charley wrote often to Edie that summer. He realized more than ever that he was nearly alone in his appreciation for art in his hometown. "I wish you were here to go sketching with me," he told her in a letter dated July 23, 1941. "I do long for somebody who will comment on something besides 'Good likeness.' It becomes **monotonous** when there's nobody around who talks your language."

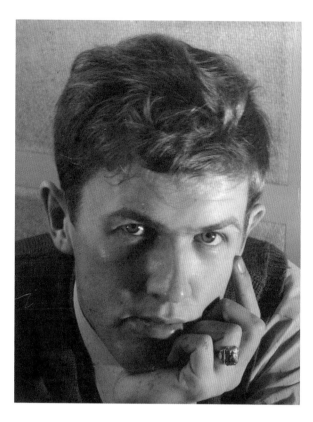

Edie McKee took this photo of Charley during their years at the Art Academy.
Courtesy of Charley Harper Art Studio

By the fall of 1941, Charley and Edie were both back at the Art Academy of Cincinnati for another year of study. They had become close friends with a group of other students, going on field trips and spending time together, sketching or socializing outside of class. Charley was finally among others who appreciated art as much as he did. He told Edie that his new friends were the nicest he'd ever had. [8]

Charley had not yet developed a style in those early years of art school. He was trying everything. Most important, he was learning to paint realistically.

When you look at Charley Harper's work today, you might not think that he was ever a realistic painter, but he was frequently quoted as saying, "I think you have got to learn to draw realistically before you can venture out on your own. You've got to know how to put everything in before you will know what you can leave out successfully."[9]

Eventually, Charley Harper would develop a unique style all his own. But first, World War II would get in the way.

DID YOU KNOW?

Water striders belong to a family of insects called **Gerridae**. Because of their ability to glide across the surface of water, they've earned a lot of interesting names, such as water skippers, pond skaters, and—as Charley grew up hearing them called—Jesus bugs. Microscopic hairs cover their entire bodies, even their legs. These hairs give them the ability to shed water, helping them maintain virtual weightlessness. Water striders prefer the still water found in ponds and puddles.[10]

3

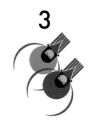

THE ARTIST BECOMES
A SOLDIER

*I remember when I was in grade school that I used to think
how lucky I was to be born after all war was ended, because
that's what the teacher always told us World War I was for. On
Armistice Day, one of the local veterans would talk to us . . . and
I'd think how nice and brave and unselfish of him to go across
the sea and fix it so that I'd never hafta be bothered with war.*

—Charley Harper[1]

O N T H E DAY before Thanksgiving 1942, Charley Harper walked in
to the post office in his hometown in West Virginia. He was not
there to mail a letter, but to see the Navy recruiter. It was his Plan B.

Charley would have preferred Plan A: to be in Cincinnati with
Edie and their friends, enjoying his third year at the Art Academy. But
war changes many people's plans, and the United States was now involved in a second world war. Like all young men, Charley had regis-
tered for the **draft,** and now, he had learned that his number was up. In
early December, just a few short days away, he would be told where to
go to join the United States Army.

Charley had never wanted to join the military, but he'd decided that if he had to enlist, he'd choose the United States Navy.[2] On that November day at the post office, he was setting into motion Plan B. He'd enlist in the navy before he was drafted into the army. But when he arrived, the recruiter told him the navy had more men than were needed, and although he could enlist, he'd be put on a waiting list. Charley enlisted on the spot.

Well, almost. First, he ran to his older sister Ruth's nearby home to take a bath. Charley knew that enlisting required a physical examination, and he suddenly realized that, because his parents were in the process of moving from one house to another, he hadn't had a proper bath for days. He made a quick excuse, ran to his sister's house, and had a good soak in her bathtub.

He passed the physical and waited, wondering who would call on him first: the army or the navy.

There was a great deal to think about during those days. Charley missed Edie and her parents, whom he'd grown to affectionately call "the Kees." He longed to be in classes in Cincinnati, growing as an artist and learning from the academy's accomplished teachers. War would only delay his career. And, of course, Charley knew that there was a very real possibility that war could do worse. It could end his career. It could end his future with Edie. It could end his life.

"I get so mad I grind my teeth when I think how well I was getting along at school and how much I was improving and how many opportunities I was having," he wrote to Edie. His next sentence, however, proved he was as selfless as the veteran he had heard speak at his school so many years before. "But that's all the griping I'm gonna do (right now) because I guess all the other guys feel the same way."[3]

On the last day of November, a letter arrived from the United States Army. Charles Harper was to report for duty on December 9, 1942. Charley still held hope that the navy would call on him before the ninth, but it didn't happen. He spent the next week getting his hair

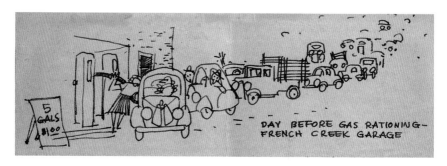

DAY BEFORE GAS RATIONING—
FRENCH CREEK GARAGE

Rationing limited access to certain products in order to supply American troops with what they needed. Charley captured the beginning of gas rationing in his hometown with this sketch in December 1942.
Courtesy of Charley Harper Art Studio. Photo by Ross Van Pelt-RVP Photography

cut, having a picture taken (at his mother's request), and going to the dentist.

He visited with his family and painted a portrait of his mother and another of his high school principal, Clifford Brake. A visit to Edie's parents' home in Cincinnati to say goodbye wasn't possible, but Charley was okay with that. It would be easier not to say goodbye at all.

On December 9, almost exactly a year after Pearl Harbor was attacked and the United States became involved in World War II, Charley became a soldier. His next letter to Edie was mailed from Camp Chaffee, Arkansas, where he would spend thirteen weeks in basic training.

Within a week of arriving, Charley wrote to Edie and asked her to send some art supplies—some pens, several **nibs**, ink, and drawing paper. Not knowing what the army would be like, he'd left all this behind. Charley soon discovered, however, that between drills, marching, obstacle courses, and **KP**, he just might find time to draw.

A few days before Christmas, invitations to eat Christmas dinner with local families were distributed around the barracks. At first, Charley didn't take one. He wasn't sure he wanted to spend the holiday with strangers. "Besides, I'm going to be so homesick that day, I'll want to be

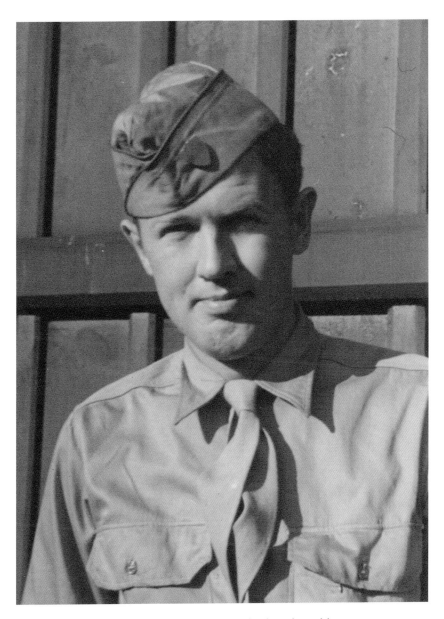

In 1942, Charley, the art student, became Charley, the soldier.
Courtesy of Charley Harper Art Studio

alone."[4] But by the next day, Charley had decided he'd go after all. It seemed those who stayed behind at camp on Christmas Day would be participating in a ten-mile hike. Suddenly dinner with strangers didn't sound so bad after all.[5]

On Christmas Day, a truck with a tarp over the top bounced across the Arkansas countryside, delivering the new young soldiers in pairs to the homes of their hosts. When Charley and a soldier named Francis were dropped off, Charley surveyed the run-down country home. He wondered if he should turn and chase the truck down, but once inside, he changed his mind. "It looked like the people were doing a good job making the best of what they had."[6]

Once dinner was served, Charley and Francis were both glad they'd come. The family's name was Kerr, and Mrs. Kerr was a wonderful cook. There was more than enough food to go around, and the meal was topped off with three kinds of cake and two kinds of pie. Charley told Edie that he thought he'd died and gone to heaven.[7] After dinner, Mr. Kerr, who was a coal miner, talked with Francis about baseball while Charley threw a football with the youngest son. The soldiers were almost sad to see the truck return to take them back to camp.

Just a few days later, Charley jumped to hear his name at mail call. Letters had been slow to arrive. So far, he had received only one from his mother and two from Edie. Charley was excited when he was handed not a letter, but a box. Inside were the art supplies he'd asked Edie to send, along with other goodies from "the gang" back in Cincinnati. Charley was so thrilled with the package, he didn't even mind that most of the candy Edie had placed inside a sock had melted into a sticky mess. He decided he could still eat the candy if he put it in his mouth, wrapper and all, and then spit out the paper.

It wasn't long before others noticed Charley's art supplies. First, soldiers asked him to draw pictures of them to send home to their loved ones. Just as in grade school, he quickly became known as the guy who could draw. He didn't mind that one bit.

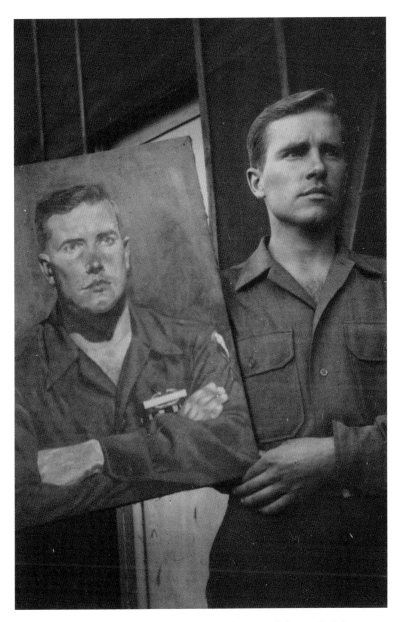

Charley sketched many fellow soldiers who gratefully mailed the
sketches home to loved ones. He painted portraits of some of his
closest friends, like Tony, pictured here with the finished painting.

Soon, the army figured out that Charley Harper, the artist, had something to offer it as well. On January 14, 1943, he wrote, "It has happened. They finally caught up with me. My past is known. Today I was called out of gunnery class by a guy who asked if I could paint signs."[8]

Charley's first assignment was to paint letters, numbers, and symbols on army trucks and motorcycles. It wasn't exactly creative work, and he was unimpressed with the supplies. The army's paintbrushes were so cheap, Charley asked to be driven to town to buy better brushes on his first afternoon on the job. For days, Charley painted signs on vehicles. He worried about what important military training he might be missing, but when the whole company woke to freezing temperatures one morning, Charley was glad he could stay inside and paint signs. While others hiked that day, Charley hand-lettered signs that read "Stop," "Road Test," and even "Please Flush." It was a direction in which he hadn't seen his art career heading, and he was quite sure it wasn't even really art. But it was painting, and his sergeant and commanding officer were pleased.

Whenever there was drawing to be done, no matter how trivial, Charley was happy to do it. Before long, he graduated from sign making to other tasks. He hand-lettered more than forty certificates of completion for soldiers who had successfully finished a mechanics course and drew a very large, detailed map of Europe so his commanding officers could more accurately follow the war. He also had fun on the staff of Camp Chaffee's company newspaper, the *Mop and Bucket*, making cartoons and other lighthearted illustrations.

Weekends sometimes offered the opportunity for Charley to sketch, draw, or paint on his own. When spring came and the weather warmed, he could be found by the creek near camp. At this point in his career, Charley's work was still mostly realistic, but as he told Edie in a letter, "I'm just dying to paint an **abstract** of a potato bug. Saw one the other day which gave me the idea, but haven't been able to find another."[9] It's likely that even Charley himself didn't know that this was the beginning of the style that would someday make his work unmistakenly recognized as Harper art.

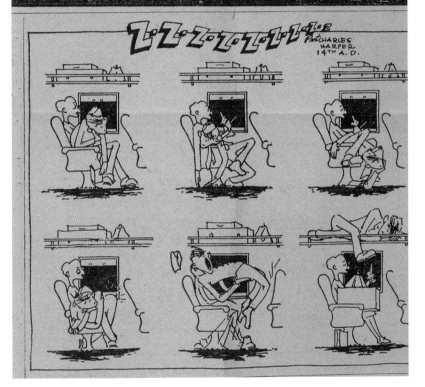

Charley pokes fun at the inconveniences of train travel.
Courtesy of Charley Harper Art Studio. Photo by Ross Van Pelt-RVP Photography

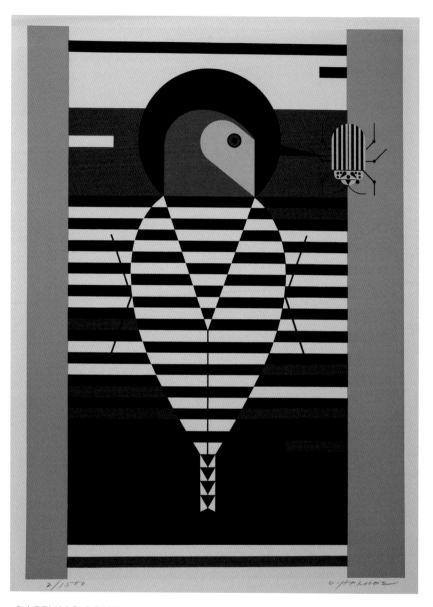

BAFFLING BELLY

Charley never did an abstract of a potato bug, as least as far as we know.
But he did put one in the mouth of this Red-Bellied Woodpecker.
Courtesy of Charley Harper Art Studio. Photo by Ross Van Pelt-RVP Photography

DID YOU KNOW?

During World War II, every letter that any United States soldier wrote was **censored** by military personnel. As a security
measure, letters were read for details that might give away a
unit's location or contain information about military opera-
tions. Sometimes, letters arrived with entire sentences blacked
out or even cut out. For this reason, some of Charley's thor-
ough accounts of his war experiences were written after his
discharge from the army, when he was once again a civilian.

4

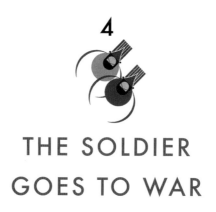

THE SOLDIER
GOES TO WAR

*I am somewhere in Belgium. It rains every day and twice on
Sundays. I'm beginning to get webbed feet.*

—Private First Class Charles Harper[1]

WHEN BASIC TRAINING ended, Charley was selected to partici-
pate in the Army Specialized Training Program (ASTP) at the
University of Delaware in Newark. The ASTP was designed to train
potential officers and to increase soldiers' technical skills. Charley was
happy to be chosen, and for a little more than nine months, he lived a
double life as both a soldier and a student. Since the ASTP required a
lot of studying, other duties were limited. With the long hikes and gun
drills of basic training behind him, Charley focused on classes and, in
his spare time, painting.

In Delaware, Charley worked hard and made lifelong friends. When
it was time to leave, some of his classmates were chosen to stay for ad-
vanced training in electrical engineering. This time, Charley was happy
not to be chosen, even though his grades were higher than those of
some who were staying. He'd had some training in electricity already,
and he found it dull.[2] Others were selected for officer candidate school.

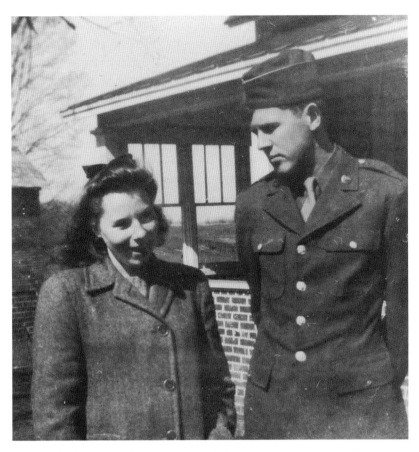

When Charley moved from one part of the country to another with the army, he usually got to spend a few days on leave, allowing him to catch up with either his family or the McKees but seldom both because of the distance between Cincinnati and his West Virginia home. In this picture, the handsome soldier reunites with his beloved Edie.

Courtesy of Charley Harper Art Studio

Charley was relieved to have dodged that honor as well. "I am quite satisfied with going back to the army as a lowly private. Privates have more friends and more time to paint."[3]

Charley and the rest of his classmates were sent to Camp Carson in Colorado for further training. This time, it wasn't technical training.

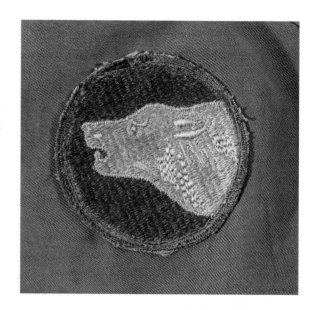

The insignia of the 104th Infantry Division, the Timberwolves. Used for informational purposes with the permission of the Army Trademark Licensing Office

The first words the commanding officers uttered to the newly arrived troops were, "You men have come to war."[4] Charley now belonged to the 414th **Infantry Regiment,** which was a part of the 104th **Infantry Division,** known as the Timberwolves. Specializing in night fighting, the Timberwolves would be on the front lines of battle. Charley's division was training for combat and would soon be overseas.

Because of his ability to draw, Charley was assigned to the **intelligence** and **reconnaissance** platoon. The duties of this platoon included scouting out the **terrain.** Because photographs took too long to shoot and then develop, soldiers with skills like Charley's were chosen to make quick, accurate sketches of the area. Training at Camp Carson was grueling. Still, Charley found time to write to Edie almost daily. In those frequent letters, he described lying on his back in mud, squirming under barbed wire while bullets flew over his head, and **foxhole**-digging practice, which seemed pointless to him because they'd just have to fill the holes in again right after digging them. He especially disliked **bayonet** practice. It made him shudder to think about using such a weapon in real combat.

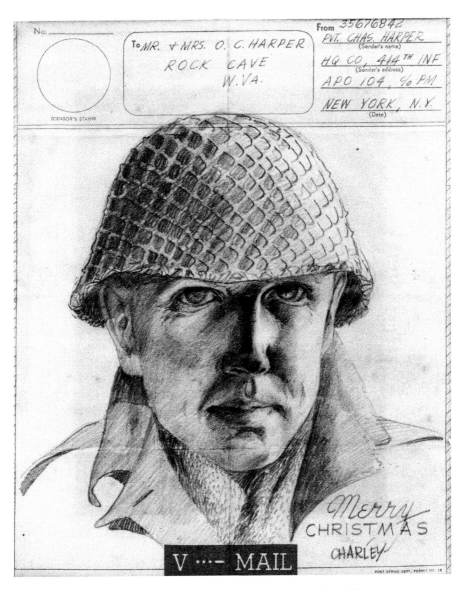

Charley sent this self-portrait home to his parents in a 1944 Christmas
V-Mail letter. It was discovered many years later by new owners of the
Harper home on Barbour Street in Buckhannon, West Virginia.
Image courtesy of the Upshur County Historical Society, Buckhannon, WV

Charley spent many evenings in the barracks sketching or painting portraits of his fellow soldiers, but Sundays offered the only free time to go away and paint what he really wanted to paint—the world around him. On more than one occasion, he was able to find time to draw the towering red rocks in the Garden of the Gods near Colorado Springs.

When the time came to board transport ships to Europe, Charley wasn't able to carry art supplies overseas with him. Fortunately, he had befriended the chaplain of his division. The chaplain knew how important it was to Charley to have drawing and painting materials with him, so he took all of Charley's art supplies in his own pack.

On September 7, 1944, Charley and the 414th Infantry Regiment landed in Cherbourg, France. Charley's division proceeded across Europe, from France to Belgium, then on to Holland, and finally to Germany. Charley did his job as a scout: setting up observation posts, planting listening devices, and reporting information back to the base camp. When he wasn't working, he'd take every opportunity to sketch, draw, or paint what he saw. In some cases, he had to work very quickly to ensure his safety, but in other situations, he could take his time to capture the details of a bombed-out building or the wrinkled face of an old German farmer.

At training camp, Charley had been able to spend Sundays painting, but war didn't take Sundays off. Every now and then, if things were quiet, Charley and the other soldiers were able to make weekend trips to neighboring towns and villages. On one trip, Charley stumbled upon "a little shop operated by two bespectacled old ladies and a big, stolid tabby cat."[5] There he bought a new art box to replace one Edie had given him back in Cincinnati. That box had survived the trip to Europe, but not the dampness of France. Charley hated to replace it, as Edie had inscribed, "Charlie is an old sweetie-pie—Edie," on the inside. With the new box in hand, Charley reluctantly buried the old one in Belgium. On that same day, he found a small store that sold art supplies, including Belgian and German paints, inks, and brushes. He was overjoyed to browse through the store. Everything there reminded him of what, and whom, he most adored.

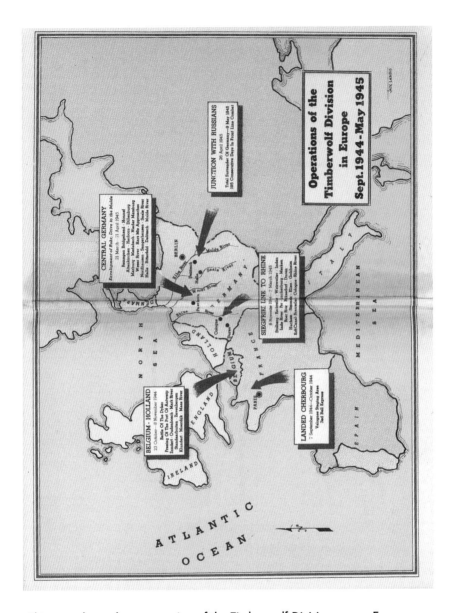

This map shows the progression of the Timberwolf Division across Europe, from Cherbourg, France, through Belgium and Holland, then on to Germany.

Map drawn by Jack Labous. Courtesy of the National Timberwolf Pups Association, Inc.

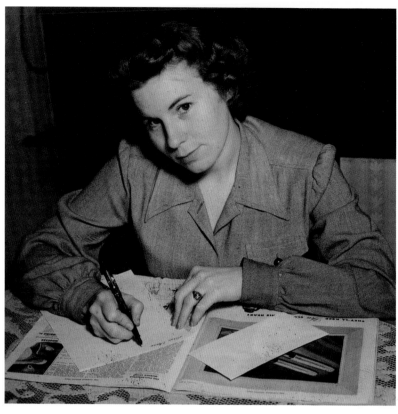

In this November 1944 photo, Edie writes a Christmas card to Charley.
Courtesy of Charley Harper Art Studio

In Belgium, the war had already torn though towns and the once-peaceful countryside. The American soldiers found the people to be very friendly. "A ragged old man stopped me and gave me a pear. Little kids hold my hands. Large signs said, 'Welcome to our **liberators**,'" Charley wrote in a letter to Edie dated October 22, 1944.

As they marched across Germany, the soldiers slept anywhere they could—abandoned buildings, homes, and even outdoors. On Christmas Eve 1944, Charley and other members of his regiment found themselves sheltered in, of all places, a stable. By the dim light of a single lantern, Charley wrote of the irony that he was "Away in a Manger."

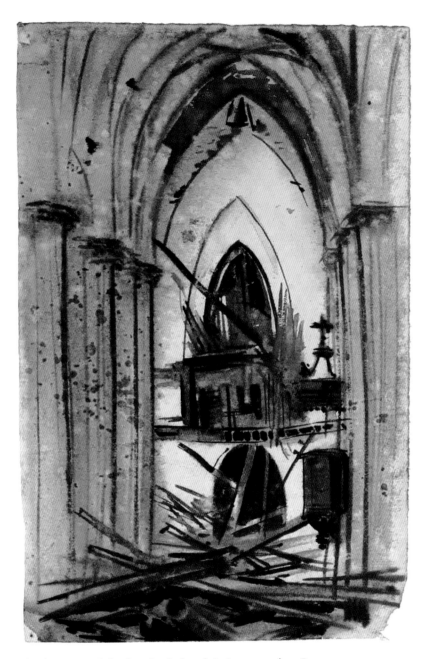

Charley painted this bombed church in Langerwehe, Germany.
Courtesy of Charley Harper Art Studio. Ross Van Pelt–RVP Photography

V-MAIL

DURING WORLD WAR II, the volume of letters sent to and from those serving in the Armed Forces so overwhelmed the United States Postal Service that they devised a new system that they called Victory Mail, or V-Mail. V-Mail used specially designed letter-and-envelope, all-in-one pages that could be obtained, with a limit of two per person, per day, from any post office.

Once a V-Mail letter was posted, postal workers in the U.S. ran it through a microfilm machine, reducing it to a tiny 16mm film negative. These compact filmstrips were lightweight and easy to send overseas in the cargo planes that carried other supplies to the troops. Once overseas, the microfilm letters were printed on small 4" x 5" cards, one-quarter the size of the original letter, and delivered.

V-Mail began on June 15, 1942, with mixed public reaction. The new system significantly reduced the number of bags filled with bulky paper mail, and it was faster and more efficient than traditional mail. V-Mail, however, had limitations. The letter writer had to stay within the margins provided on the V-Mail paper and limit his or her correspondence to just a single page. No enclosures, such as cherished photographs, were permitted, and legible penmanship was a must. Remember, the reader would see the letter at one-fourth the size of the original.

To learn more about V-Mail, visit the Smithsonian's National Postal Museum Victory Mail online exhibit, https://postalmuseum.si.edu/victorymail/index.html.[10]

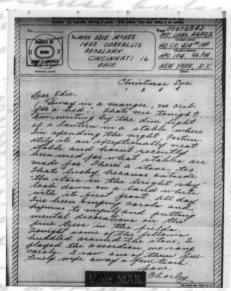

Some of Charley's letters to Edie were sent via V-Mail
Courtesy of Charley Harper Art Studio

That night, while families in the United States gathered around Christmas trees, those American soldiers huddled around a stove as Charley played an accordion he'd found and everyone sang carols. It was an emotional night for everyone, filled with fear and homesickness.

Back in his training days, Charley had become known as "squeaky clean." Unlike many of his fellow soldiers, Charley didn't smoke, or drink beer or liquor, and he kept his language clean. He took a fair amount of ribbing from the guys, especially when he'd stay back in the barracks to write or paint while the others went to bars or parties. Despite their teasing, the other soldiers respected Charley for sticking to what he believed.

On New Year's Day 1945, some of Charley's friends asked him to help them reform their ways and hold them accountable if they slipped. Charley was amused as he shared in that day's letter to Edie, "One of the fellows who had a tendency to become sewer-mouthed is going to deposit one mark (German currency worth ten cents) with me every time he cusses. Will send all I collect home to his wife who'll put it in their son's college fund. He was playing cards last night and I collected the first remittance a few minutes after 12:00."

January in Germany was frigid. If he was lucky, Charley would be called upon for a drawing assignment. Once, he was asked to create four drawings for a brief history of his division. He was given a warm office in which to work and a radio to listen to. He made the work last three days.

In Germany, the **civilians** were not always as accepting of the **Allied soldiers** as the people in the rest of Europe had been. Some were followers of Adolf Hitler, the leader of the Nazi party; others were his victims. In either case, their lives and homes had been torn apart by the war, and they were left to piece together an existence amid the rubble. Once, Charley and some other soldiers found a small dog who liked to ride on the hood of their Army jeep, proudly barking at everyone they passed. "Every German we met grinned at us," Charley wrote. "For the first time in my experience, we seemed to have a common bond. Maybe our ambassadors should have been Cocker Spaniels."[6]

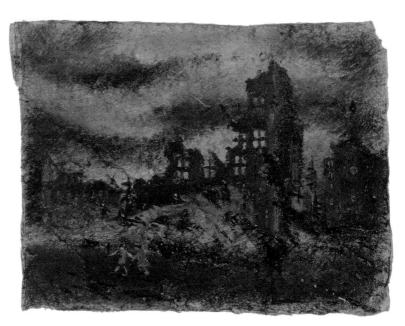

STROLL THROUGH OBLIVION, 1944–45, gouache and oil
Charley painted this on the lid of an ammunition box.
Courtesy of Charley Harper Art Studio. Photo by Ross Van Pelt-RVP Photography

News from home usually came slowly, but on April 12, 1945, the news of President Franklin Delano Roosevelt's death spread quickly among the troops. Charley recalled what a shock it had been, as he and his fellow soldiers had placed a great deal of confidence in their **commander in chief.**

The other news that spread like wildfire came on May 7, 1945. V-E Day, or Victory-in-Europe Day, came as the result of the surrender of the Nazi forces. It signaled the end of World War II in Europe, but the war continued in Japan. Though there was much celebrating all over Europe, including within Charley's division, people remained cautious. "Somehow we aren't as happy here as we perhaps should be," Charley wrote. "We know it's only half over and wonder if our part is just half done."[7]

Luckily, for Charley and the other members of the 104th Infantry Division, 414th Infantry Regiment, their part in the war was finished.

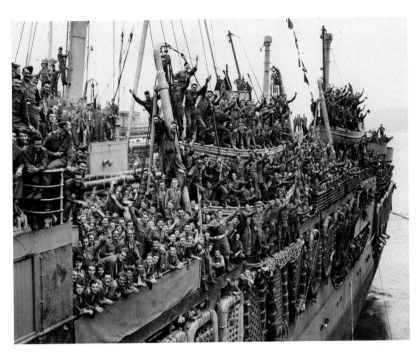

Charley arrived back in the United States aboard the SS *John Ericsson* in an earlier sailing, just about a month before this picture was taken.

Ravenna, A., photographer. (1945)*Troops of the 20th Armored Division and units of the 9th Army whoop it up between raindrops as the SS* John Ericsson *nears Pier 84, North River/*World Telegram & Sun *photo by Al Ravenna.* August 6. [Image] Retrieved from the Library of Congress, https://www.loc.gov/item/2008680587/

On July 2, 1945, the USS *John Ericsson* left France with Charley Harper on board. The ship arrived in New York on July 11. Charley was back in the United States, but it would be months before he would be home.

At Camp San Luis Obispo in California, Charley's army service continued. His sister Reta had moved to San Francisco two years earlier, so Charley enjoyed frequent visits with her. The Japanese surrendered in mid-August 1945, but V-J Day was officially celebrated on September 2, 1945. With victory in Japan came the official end of World War II and the end of Charley's worries that he might have to return to combat. Discharges were determined by a point system, however, and Charley wasn't among the first to be allowed to go home.

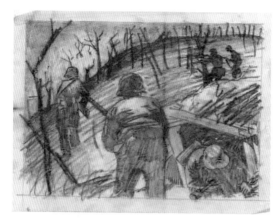

The cover sketch
Charley mailed home
to Edie.
Courtesy of Charley Harper
Art Studio

The February 1946
cover of *Infantry
Journal.*
Courtesy of the Association
of the U.S. Army

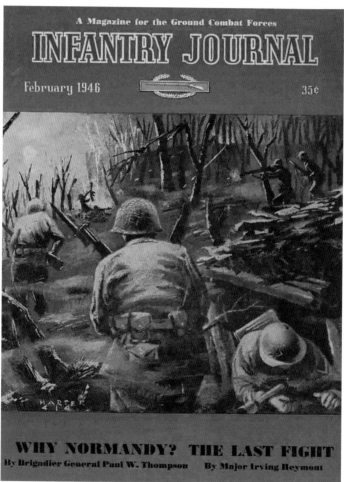

A Magazine for the Ground Combat Forces

INFANTRY JOURNAL

February 1946   35¢

WHY NORMANDY?   THE LAST FIGHT
By Brigadier General Paul W. Thompson   By Major Irving Heymont

Peacetime in the army was a lot more relaxed than wartime had been, especially **stateside**. In addition to the normal army patrols and duties, Charley was put to work making signs, lettering, and painting portraits. Fortunately, he also had time to paint by the Pacific Ocean, to go bowling with Reta and her friends, to see movies by the dozens, and to read biographies of great artists, some of which were mailed to Charley from Edie in Ohio.

In September 1945, Charley was called upon to create illustrations and covers for *Infantry Journal*, a monthly army magazine. He would turn in the finished illustrations and send his preliminary sketches home to Edie. About these combat drawings, Charley commented that the subject matter wasn't very enjoyable and he questioned that they contributed anything of importance to the art world, but he liked the challenges he faced as he drew night scenes. It provided good experience working with light and shadow. The fact that these maneuvers took place at night was the very reason the army needed Charley's illustration: photographers could not capture the events in poor light. Another perk of doing the *Infantry Journal* illustrations? It got him out of KP duty indefinitely.[8]

Finally, on November 6, 1945, Charley penned the words he'd longed to write. "This is V-Me Day. I'm a civilian. I'm one of you."[9]

5

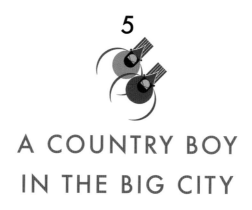

A COUNTRY BOY
IN THE BIG CITY

It has suddenly occurred to me that I've done something wrong in coming so far from all my friends. I feel like the city mouse, except I'm the country mouse.

—Charley Harper[1]

CHARLEY HARPER WAS happily reunited with his family and Edie McKee in November 1945. He'd served his country for two years, ten months, and twenty-nine days, and at last, he was free to pursue the art career he'd always dreamed of. Many years later, Charley would look back on his time in the service and reflect upon how those years affected his art:

> While I was constantly assailed by the senselessness and over-whelming horror of war, I was also fascinated by the series of devastation we encountered constantly in Germany, and I found time to make a large portfolio of on-the-spot sketches and paintings. I see now that this was a fruitful training period for me as an artist (although I don't recommend it as a substitute for art school) because it taught me to grasp the important elements of a scene quickly and put them down with a minimum of detail.[2]

The **GI** Bill, more formally known as the Serviceman's Readjustment Act of 1944, was a law passed by Congress that provided benefits to returning soldiers. One of those benefits was college tuition. This meant that Charley could study art anywhere he chose, and it seemed logical to go where some of the best artists, art galleries, and art museums were—New York City. Even as he packed to leave West Virginia for New York, Charley was having doubts. Where would he live in New York? He'd inquired about a place to stay and he'd heard nothing. Maybe he should remain in West Virginia, get a job, and make some money. Better yet, maybe he should propose to Edie, and they could start a life together in Cincinnati. Eventually, he decided that so many people had praised his art, he just had to see if he could live up to their expectations. "The next letter you get from me," he told Edie the night before he left, "will probably be written from my private bench in Central Park."[3]

Charley was joking, of course, but his prediction nearly came true. He arrived in New York City by train at seven o'clock in the morning on the tenth of January 1946. The Art Students League of New York, where he would enroll in classes, had suggested housing, but none of those boardinghouses had rooms available. He walked for hours, stopping at hotels and rentals, only to be turned away at each one. He had the address of some army friends and, fortunately, he was able to stay with them for the night. Already, he hated the city. It was big and noisy and it made him uncomfortable.[4]

The next day, after walking what seemed like a thousand more miles, he found a room on West 103rd Street. It was small and dark and empty, but at five dollars per week, the price was right. His sixty-five dollars per month from the GI Bill wasn't expected for a month or two. Once he was alone in his new room, though, Charley began having doubts again. Surely, once he was enrolled at the Art Students League and taking the classes he'd been longing for, he'd feel differently.

Enrolling at the League was challenging. When he arrived there to sign up for classes, Charley was told that since he was a GI, he'd need a letter from the Veterans Administration. He headed out to get the letter. Hours later, he returned to the League to learn that all but two classes were already full. Neither was one of the classes he had wanted, but he signed up for them anyway. He was in New York City to study art, so he might as well take the classes and hope for better ones next term. That evening, like most others, he wrote to Edie. He confessed that coming to New York wasn't turning out to be the adventure he had anticipated.[5]

Charley was enrolled in a modern painting class in the afternoon, and, in the evening, he would learn life drawing, painting, and composition. Both classes were to be taught by well-known artists, but Charley soon learned that the instructors showed up only when they wanted to. Most of the time, monitors led the classes. Both classes were so crowded that Charley had a hard time finding a spot to work. He was often far away from the model he was supposed to be drawing. "And I thought the *John Ericsson* was crowded,"[6] he exclaimed, referring to the ship that had brought the troops back from Europe.

Back in his room, Charley waited days for the landlady to turn on the hot water. His living conditions were unlike any he'd encountered outside of wartime. The floor and walls weren't clean and the lighting was too dim to work by. For weeks, Charley debated if he should stay in New York City or if he should go home. He even wrote to the Art Academy of Cincinnati to inquire if room was available in classes there. One day, he'd write to Edie saying he'd decided to stay for a least a month. The next day, he'd declare he was only giving it a few more days. "I think the only reason I've stayed this long is that I've had this planned for so long that, even though I'm dazed with disappointment, I just can't drop it like a hot potato. I feel like a balloon that just ran into a pin,"[7] he wrote.

Pride and fear of regret were two more forces in play. Charley was worried that Edie, her parents, and perhaps even his family would see him as a failure if he lasted only a few weeks in New York City. He didn't want to look back and wonder what would have happened to his art career if he'd stayed.

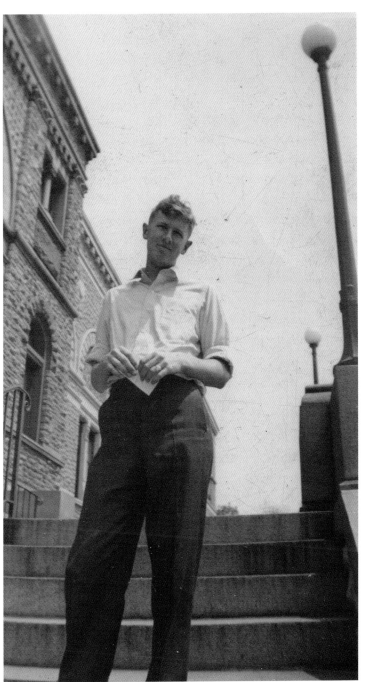

**Charley Harper
as a young art
student.**
Courtesy of
Charley Harper
Art Studio

Finally, at the end of January, Charley reached a turning point. It happened in his evening class when the instructor, Italian artist Louis Bosa, praised Charley's drawing. He indicated to the whole class that what Charley was doing was something not everyone could do. Bosa marveled at Charley's diverse styles. "You are searching for something," Bosa told him. "And you will find it."[8] In what might have been a somewhat prophetic statement, Bosa took a look at Charley's landscapes (which were still primarily realistic) and said they had an "unreal reality" to them that Charley "could develop into a fine personal style."[9] Charley laughed when he shared the story with Edie, saying he wasn't sure whether to doubt the artist or go celebrate. Charley decided to celebrate that night by spending ten precious cents on applesauce cake and milk. He'd made a decision: He still hated New York City, but he'd stay until the end of the term in May.

Over the next several months, Charley made new friends in class and reunited with a few other GIs who were also in school in New York. He used the opportunity to take in as many art shows as the city could offer. He visited every museum he could, including the Metropolitan Museum of Art, though the museum itself left him unimpressed. It was so large that he became lost inside, and he wasn't fond of all the ornate, gold frames.[10]

By March, the little enthusiasm Charley had mustered for the Art Students League was fading. The instructor in his afternoon class, abstract artist Vaclav Vytlacil, said Charley's work looked "tired,"[11] and Charley couldn't argue. He felt drained of energy and inspiration. He constantly compared the League to his classes at the Art Academy of Cincinnati, where he felt the instruction was far superior. Charley was tired of everything: his dark, dirty room, the Veterans Administration hassles that still prevented any GI Bill funds from reaching him, eating only two meals a day to save money, and the unfriendly people around him. City people were not the same as the folks he'd known back home in West Virginia or even in Cincinnati. Country folks "wouldn't think of riding nose-to-nose with you on the subway without at least saying 'It's a nice day' or 'Do you think the rain'll spoil the rhubarb?'"[12] he wrote to Edie in late January. Many of his letters began the same way: *Dear Ediepie. I'm sick.* Sometimes, Charley was speaking of his homesickness and longing for family and friends, but for weeks he was actually ill, battling an eye infection likely due to poor nutrition.

Fortunately, March brought a visitor to New York City, and that visitor brought some life back to Charley's days. Charley held his breath as news of a possible nationwide railroad **strike** threatened the arrival of his beloved Edie, but on Saturday, March 9, 1946, Charley was at Penn Station to meet Edie's train from Cincinnati.

Edie stayed a week in New York City, bunking with a mutual friend and enjoying the New York art scene. With Edie, Charley revisited his favorite **galleries**, shows, and museums. New York agreed with Charley a bit more when Edie was around. When she left, Charley was quick to tell her how much her visit had inspired him. Apparently, Edie had set Charley straight regarding his attitude. "I feel more cheerful since you pointed out in no uncertain terms that I'm making a **worry wart** of myself for no good reason,"[13] he wrote before her train could have even deposited her back in Cincinnati.

Charley's improved outlook carried over to his work. One evening in class, Bosa commented that Charley's art was different and more exciting than it had been. Motivated once again, Charley began producing sketches and paintings at a pace that surprised even him. "I did more abstracts in Vyt's (Vytlacil's) class. I'm going to shock him with quantity this week,"[14] he told Edie.

Charley continued to visit art galleries, and even tried to get some of his work into a few. But the galleries were only interested in showing what they could sell, and Charley did not want to put his art up for sale, especially the work he'd done during the war.

Once, Charley and a friend visited a gallery displaying the work of well-known artist Milton Avery. Charley was struck by the simplicity of the exhibit. He studied the way the artist used shape and color to create something very different from what others were painting at the time. Later in class, Vytlacil praised Charley for presenting "simple, pleasing shapes in pleasing colors."[15] He used Charley's painting as an

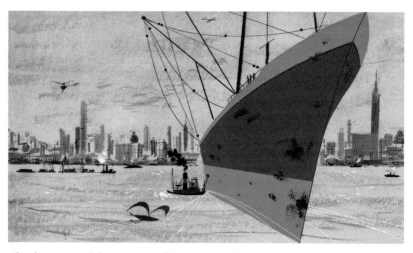

Charley painted this picture of the New York harbor after he was no longer living in the city. But he may have sketched this or similar scenes while he was a student in the city. He and his friends spent time painting in Central Park and on Long Island in the spring of 1946.
Courtesy of Charley Harper Art Studio

example for the class, saying that instead of painting complex forms, they should consider what Charley had done with just a few shapes and colors. Charley was sure he'd been influenced by what he had seen in the Milton Avery exhibition.[16]

Spring came, and with it, the end of Charley's financial worries. His GI money arrived the same day as a check for his *Infantry Journal* cover illustration. In addition, a book about the Timberwolves, titled, *Timberwolf Tracks,* was being planned, and Charley had been asked to provide some illustrations for it. The best news of all, however, was that the Timberwolves' commander, Major General Terry de la Mesa Allen, had contacted the *Infantry Journal* asking to buy Charley's original cover drawing for his personal collection of Timberwolf **memorabilia.** Charley could name his price, the general said. Charley sold him the drawing for fifty dollars.

Charley finished his semester at the Art Students League at the end of May and signed up for the fall term before leaving New York City to

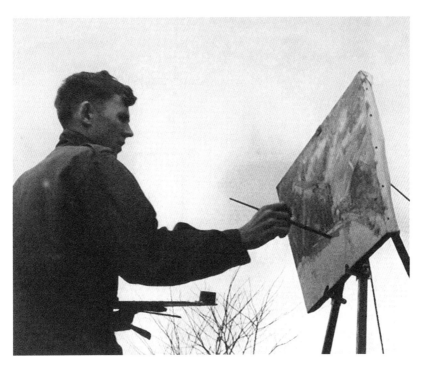

Charley's early connections with nature on his family's farm served as a foundation for the art he would create as he became older.
Courtesy of Charley Harper Art Studio

spend the summer back at home. He never did return, though. Five months in the Big Apple had been enough for the country boy from West Virginia.

On one of his first days home, Charley visited his grandfather's abandoned farm. He sat in the old chicken house and painted a watercolor of the empty house. When he returned home that evening, he wrote these words to Edie:

> At dusk the night things take over and fill the hollow with chirps and squeaks and rasps. This is one homecoming I'm enjoying especially much. When I think of hot, narrow streets filled with screaming, squirming kids, smelling armpits on crowded subways, and rooms with 25-watt bulbs, cockroaches and no chairs, I want to be a hick all my life.[17]

6

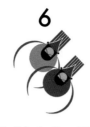

FINDING THAT
CHARLEY HARPER STYLE

*There's a pinch of Dr. Seuss, a sprinkling of Dr. Doolittle,
and maybe a moral or two lifted from the pages of Aesop in
Harper's world view.*

—Todd Wilkinson, *Wildlife Art News*[1]

CHARLEY HARPER RETURNED from New York to finish train-ing at the Art Academy of Cincinnati. Edie had graduated while Charley was serving in World War II. In addition to painting and draw-ing, she had learned the art of photography, including **film processing**. She had no trouble landing a job as a photographer with the Army Corps of Engineers. When Charley returned, Edie also took more art classes at the Academy. Charley and Edie were painting, drawing, and pursuing their art careers together once more.

At the end of his last year of study, the Art Academy declared Charley their most outstanding student. He surpassed sixty other ap-plicants to win the first Stephen H. Wilder Traveling Scholarship, which included a generous cash prize, a semester's tuition, and an opportunity to travel. Charley liked to joke that since he had money to travel but no car, he proposed to Edie, whose father had an old Chevrolet they could

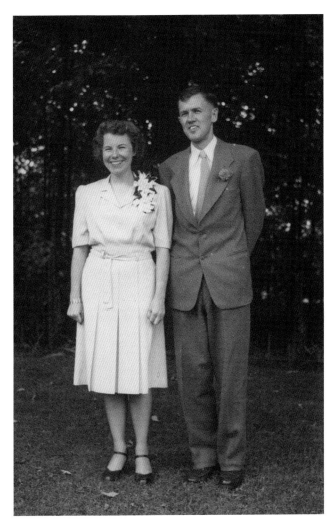

Mr. and Mrs.
Charley Harper on
their wedding day
at the home of
Mr. and Mrs.
George McKee,
August 9, 1947.
Courtesy of Charley
Harper Art Studio

use.[2] In reality, Charley's affection for Edie was greater than his need for her father's car. In the nearly seven years since Charley had met Edie on their first day of art school, the two had spent as much time together as they possibly could. And when circumstances and distance separated them, they had exchanged letters almost daily.

On a very warm Saturday in August 1947, Charley and Edie were married in the McKees' living room.

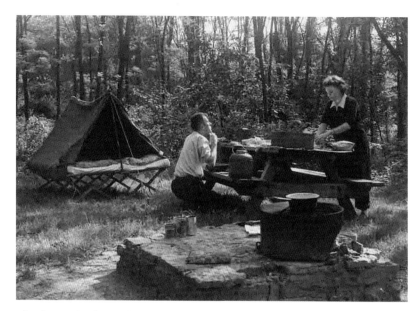

Charley and Edie each documented their honeymoon trip in their own ways. The photo was probably taken by Edie using a tripod with a timer.

The watercolor painting was included by Charley in an August 28, 1947, letter to a friend.

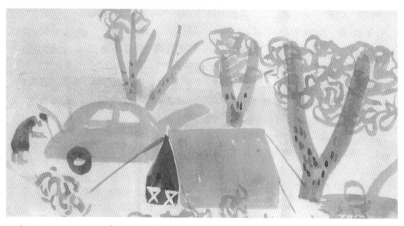

Both images courtesy of Charley Harper Art Studio

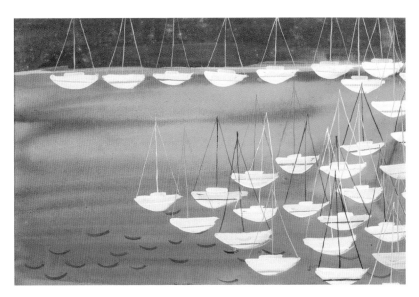

BOATS IN HARBOR

Charley's minimal style is beginning to emerge in this 1947 watercolor painted during their honeymoon.

Courtesy of Charley Harper Art Studio

Soon they were off on a honeymoon adventure, driving west across the United States, sketching and painting during the day, and camping at night with two cots and a pup tent. Sometimes they just found a nice spot along the highway, pulled off, and pitched their tent for the night. Edie had her camera along and when the sun went down, she would duck into her "**darkroom**"—under a tent of blankets—to check her film.

Edie wrote to her friend Marjorie Keil, "So far we like the ocean best of anything we've seen. Every time we watch it we can hardly stop looking and go home. When we aren't drooling over '**la mer**,' we are practicing to be **beachcombers**. Will probably get to the place where we will have to leave our luggage to make room for the sticks, stones, and shells."[3]

Over the next several months, Edie and Charley drove all the way to California and back east to Florida, stopping at parks and rivers, drawing as they went. "We'd go out and get our eyes full and then come

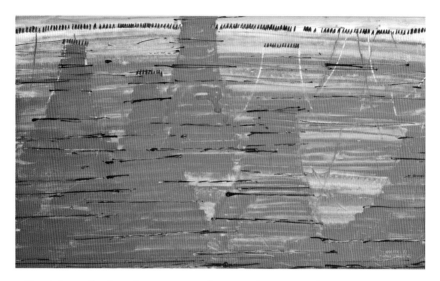

This is how Charley chose to paint the Grand Canyon when he and Edie visited there on their honeymoon.
Courtesy of Charley Harper Art Studio. Photo by Ross Van Pelt-RVP Photography

back to 'our little home' and empty them making pictures,"[4] Edie wrote. One of their favorite art instructors from Cincinnati, Maybelle Stamper, had moved into a primitive grass hut on Captiva Island, off the Florida coast, so they stopped to visit her as well.

While on their honeymoon, Charley and Edie enjoyed painting together, but they also painted separately. Sometimes they sat in the same spot and painted the same scene, then compared how each had decided to represent what they both had seen. Charley was giving a lot of thought to painting more simply, with flat and simple shapes. When he and Edie reached the mountains, he knew he was on to something. "I couldn't get a Rocky Mountain on a piece of paper without simplifying it,"[5] Charley said.

Once they were back in Cincinnati, Charley found a job as a **commercial artist** at a downtown art studio, the C. H. Schaten Studio. He was miserable. The studio's clients would prescribe just exactly what they wanted drawn for their advertisements. Charley had to draw housewives joyfully opening refrigerator doors or smiling while holding soap. He was still drawing realistically—perhaps too realistically—as his housewives sometimes had wrinkles or appeared not to be enjoying their chores. The company decided to put Charley to work on something different—creating detailed drawings of **cysts** for a medical brochure.

"It was the most successful failure of my life," Charley said later, "because it made me realize that in order to succeed as an illustrator, I must offer something besides realism. . . . I began searching for something peculiarly me—a style, a technique, a point of view—and gradually it emerged."[6]

Even though it wasn't enjoyable, Charley stuck with the studio job and did **freelance** work in the evenings. His freelance work with *Ford Times*, a magazine published by the Ford Motor Company, helped Charley find that "something peculiar." He had created several illustrations for the magazine's interior, but in 1951, Charley painted his first *Ford Times* cover.

Readers of the magazine liked the cover image so much, the *Ford Times* asked Charley for more fish illustrations. After eight fish, the art director asked Charley to draw birds for an article written by E. B. White, who had just recently published *Charlotte's Web*. Charley set up a feeding station in order to observe birds in their natural state. He quickly learned that, even at a feeder, birds never pose for portraits the way people do, so he used photographs of birds instead. His eight bird paintings were as popular as his fish paintings had been, and soon *Ford Times* began to offer prints of Charley's illustrations for $4.95 apiece, or about $48 each in today's terms. However, collectors hoping to own one of these prints today can expect to pay more than $1,000.

Those prints were serigraphs, handmade by Charley and Edie in the McKees' basement, where the couple had set up both their home and studio after returning from their honeymoon. Serigraphy is a complex and time-consuming process in which a synthetic mesh "silk" is stretched across a frame and colored inks are forced through holes cut in a stencil. The paper on the other side of the mesh catches the ink. Each color must be done separately, with drying time in between applications.

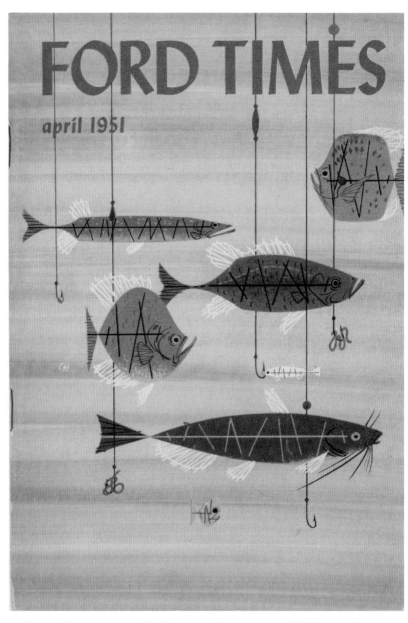

In this *Ford Times* cover, Charley is just beginning to shift from realistic painting to what he would eventually call "minimal realism."

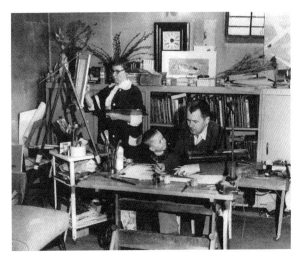

Brett worked along-side his parents from an early age, shown here in the basement studio at the McKee home, around 1956.
Courtesy of Charley Harper Art Studio. Photo by Ross Van Pelt-RVP Photography

Despite its difficulties, Charley believed silkscreen printing was the very best way to produce prints of his work. "Of all the printing processes, it provides the most intimate contact between artist and viewer,"[7] he explained. So, Edie would mix the paint colors, and Charley would cut the stencils, and together they would make the prints to fill the orders that came to them from *Ford Times.*

Once, when Charley was still wrestling with just how much detail and precision he should use in his drawings, he painted the words, "Be Sloppy," on a piece of paper and hung it over his drawing table as a reminder to himself to work a little more "loosely." The next day, he was surprised to find his mother-in-law had added something to the message. "You are," she'd written below his words.

Edie's father had battled **multiple sclerosis,** and the disease worsened while Edie was in art school. Having Edie and Charley around was a big help to both Mr. and Mrs. McKee. In 1953, the household grew by one more with the birth of Brett, Charley and Edie's only child, and the McKees' only grandchild.

It took some time, but Charley finally settled into a style uniquely his own, a style that others instantly recognize even today. He called it "**minimal realism,**"[8] and he arrived at it by going back to one of the most basic drawing principles he'd learned in art school: straight and

EDIE THE ARTIST

WHO WAS THIS young lady named Edith McKee? The only child of George and Mabel McKee, Edie was born in Kansas in 1922. The family lived for a while in Missouri before coming to Cincinnati, Ohio, so Mr. McKee could work for Procter & Gamble, a manufacturer of soap and other household products. Living in Cincinnati during high school meant that Edie had access to the Art Academy of Cincinnati's weekend classes. As a teenager, Edie was already showing great promise as an artist. In 1940, she applied to and was accepted as a student at the Art Academy.

Even though women weren't drafted to serve in World War II, many women put their dreams of a career or starting a family on hold to contribute to the war effort. Edie was no exception. Her outstanding photography skills landed her a job with the Army Corps of Engineers, photographing dams and cement samples. She would later joke that taking pictures of cement was just as dull as it sounded.

Edie was every bit as much of an artist as her husband. In addition to being an accomplished painter and photographer, she sculpted, made jewelry, and was a critical part of the Harper silkscreening team. But Edie was not as celebrated in the art world as Charley. Perhaps it was because of the societal rules of the 1940s and 1950s, when women were expected to work at home and care for their families. Edie did just that, in her own way. She spent a lifetime working alongside Charley, raising Brett, and making the Harper home a sanctuary of creativity.

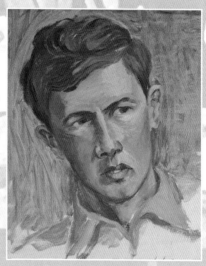

Edie painted this portrait of Charley.
Courtesy of Charley Harper Art Studio.
Photo by Ross Van Pelt-RVP Photography

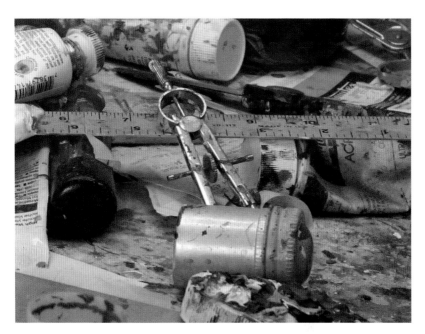

Drafting tools helped Charley achieve his flat, hard-edged shapes.
Photo by the author

curved lines. "I don't try to put everything in—I try to leave everything out. I think flat, hard-edge, and simple,"[9] he said. Careful use of color and the overlapping of shapes helped him create depth without shading. Solid colors with just enough lines to help identify the subject seemed to work beautifully.

Charley found that mechanical drawing tools were some of the best to achieve the effect he was after. **Compasses** made perfect circles. Rulers made straight lines. **French curves**, **T-squares**, and triangles became old standbys. Charley often told others that, without a ruler, he couldn't draw a straight line.[10]

In 1958, Charley and Edie bought a wooded five-acre plot of land. It would become their own bit of wilderness tucked in the middle of a growing Cincinnati neighborhood called Finneytown. There they built their home and studio, a pair of modern structures that blended with the beech trees and hillside and were filled with natural light. Quite by accident, the ladybug became the Harper family symbol. Charley was

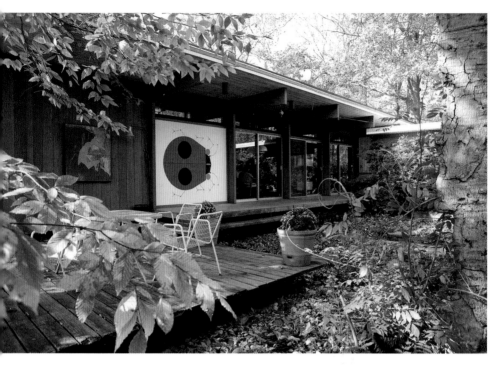

The Harper house sported a large ladybug, evidence of its inhabitants' love of nature.
Courtesy of Charley Harper Art Studio. Photo by Ross Van Pelt-RVP Photography

putting together an exhibit of his work and wanted to add something bright to the collection. He painted his first ladybug. Soon afterward, the Harpers began sending ladybug-themed Christmas cards, and their trademark stuck.

In 1960, Golden Press, a New York City publishing company, asked Charley to do all the illustrations for *The Giant Golden Book of Biology*. This was no small task. The book was nearly one hundred pages long, and many pages contained multiple drawings. It took Charley a year to complete the work. "I had no background in nature study, only a farm boy's familiarity with it,"[11] he said. "I wasn't a star at biology in high school or college. I did pretty well in lab class when I had to draw pictures."[12]

The Giant Golden Book of

BIOLOGY

An Introduction to the Science of Life

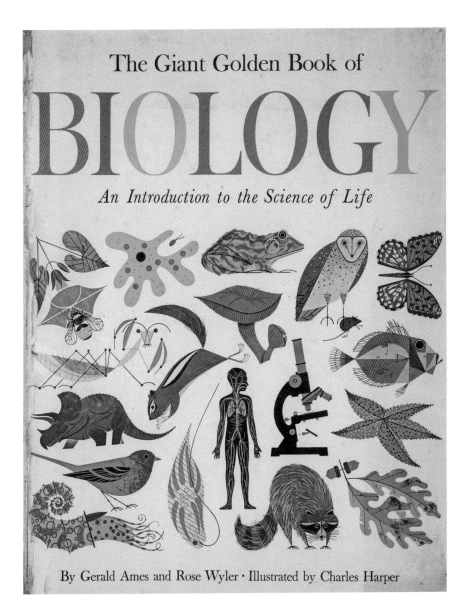

By Gerald Ames and Rose Wyler · Illustrated by Charles Harper

Illustrating this book would do three things: (1) solidify Charley's desire to focus on nature subjects; (2) introduce Charley's work to the masses; and (3) make the subject of biology fascinating to young readers everywhere.

Charley took the time to learn about each organism, plant, or animal before creating the illustrations. The book was a success. He was hired to illustrate more books, and he decided it was time to leave his job as a commercial artist and focus on the creative projects that others were asking him to do.

Ford Times continued to contact Charley regularly with assignments. Charley liked the **art director**, Arthur Lougee, saying he gave him "interesting assignments and a lot of freedom."[13] In addition to regular work, *Ford Times* also promoted the sale of Harper's prints in nearly every issue, making it easy for fans of his illustrations to order directly from Charley and Edie. The magazine stopped publication in 1993, but it was largely responsible for bringing Charley Harper's work to countless households in America for decades.

DID YOU KNOW?

In the March 1962 issue of *Ford Times* magazine, Charley illustrated an article about kite flying written by Jane Yolen. The article, titled "Fly a Kite with the Champion," was about her father's impressive adventures with giant and powerful kites. Charley chose to accompany Jane's story with three vivid illustrations of mountain, meadow, and beach kites.[14] Jane's first picture book would release the following year, and she would go on to become one of the most prolific and beloved authors of children's literature, winning dozens of awards, including the Society of Children's Book Writers and Illustrators' Golden Kite Award and the National Jewish Book Award for Children's Literature.

7

WILD ABOUT CHARLEY

How can you make shapes of animals with the shapes and they aren't even the shape of the animals?

—Andrea, Grade 5, Springdale Elementary[1]

IS A CARDINAL really a teardrop? A seal pup a circle? A bullfrog a heart?

Charley would see them that way. When he looked at any creature, he considered how he would reduce what he saw to its simplest form. "When I start to paint a bird," he said. "I don't count all the feathers in the wings—I just count the wings."[2]

After illustrating *The Giant Golden Book of Biology* and then *The Animal Kingdom*, Charley was hooked on creating art that featured wildlife. He could see in nature everything he loved about art: patterns, form, color, and texture. Having found great satisfaction in illustrating all kinds of wildlife, Charley decided to commit all his time to working with nature subjects.

Charley's fascination with animal behavior led him to become a naturalist as well as an artist. Charley was not interested in drawing any animal outside of its natural habitat. He wanted people to learn something about where the animal lives and how it behaves. Often, he could be found in a canoe on a lake with a clipboard in hand or standing quietly in a meadow, binoculars poised, to observe a bird feeding

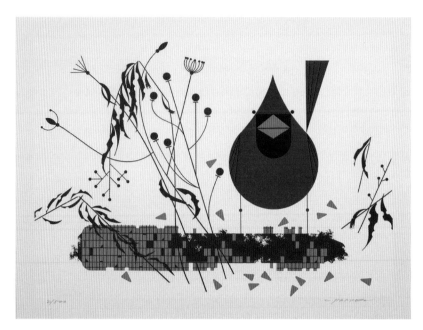

RED AND FED

These three paintings demonstrate Charley's ability to take any subject down to its simplest form.
Courtesy of Charley Harper Art Studio. Photo by Ross Van Pelt-RVP Photography

WHITECOAT

FROG EAT FROG

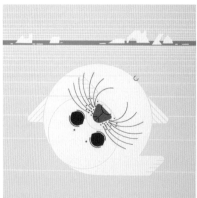

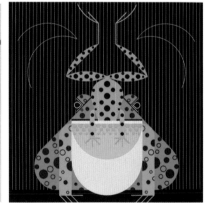

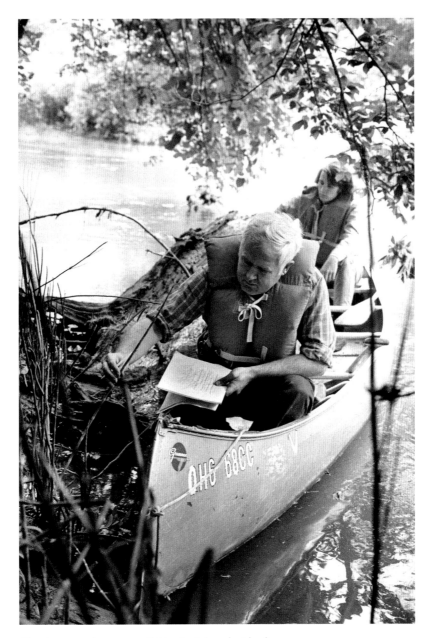

Charley wasn't a naturalist by training, but he became one.
Courtesy of Charley Harper Art Studio

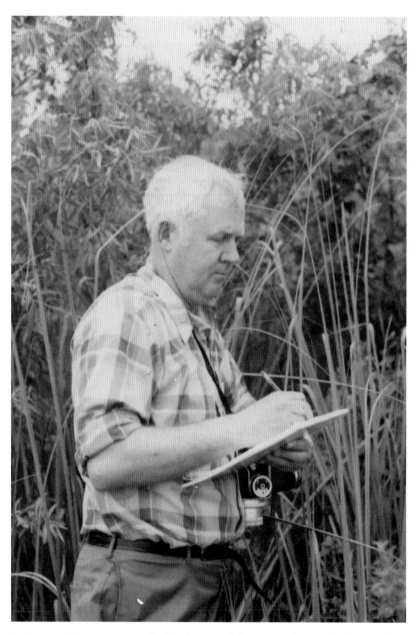

Before painting any animal, Charley carefully researched its habitat and behavioral characteristics.

Courtesy of Charley Harper Art Studio

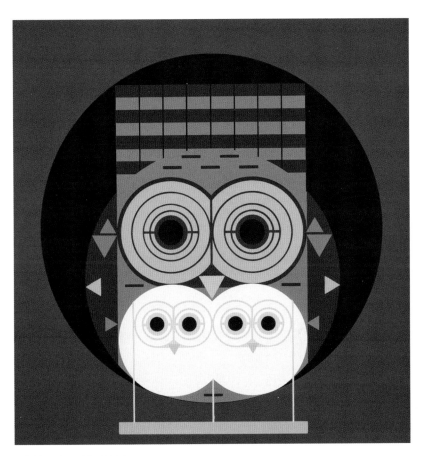

FAMILY OWLBUM

Courtesy of Charley Harper Art Studio. Photo by Ross Van Pelt-RVP Photography

its young. As Charley and Edie's son Brett grew, he became a frequent companion to Charley, both in the studio and on research expeditions. Taking after his parents, Brett was becoming, according to Charley, an "ardent **conservationist** and conscientious craftsman."[3]

Of course, Charley realized it wasn't possible to travel to every continent and observe every animal in its natural habitat, so he had to be resourceful. To get different perspectives, he used as many books as he could find on each subject he drew. He visited natural history museums to view exhibits of animal bones, teeth, and skins. He studied

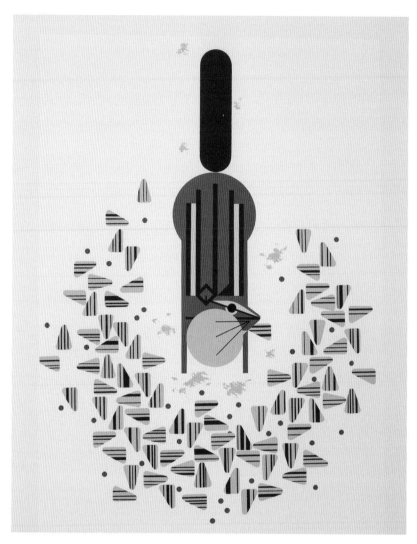

CHEEKY CHIPPY
Courtesy of Charley Harper Art Studio. Photo by Ross Van Pelt-RVP Photography

photographs and realistic paintings of animals for reference. While he truly loved to spend time outdoors, he found it much easier to draw animals from guidebooks. "They hold still there,"[4] he said.

Charley was always careful to steer clear of **anthropomorphism,** or giving animals humanlike characteristics. His animal subjects would

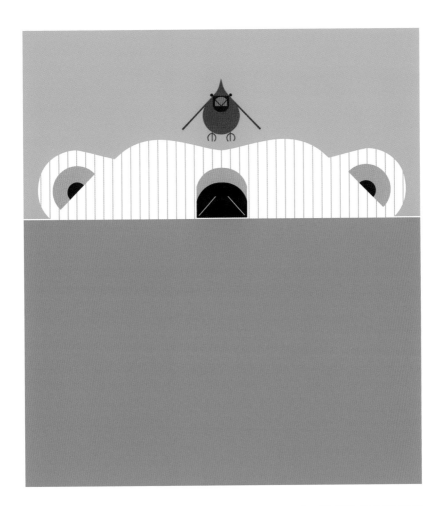

SCARY SCENARIO

Completed in 2006, this was the last painting Charley Harper created. On his desk rests the evidence of his hard work: an encyclopedia, sketches, paint-covered drafting tools, and his eyeglasses.

Courtesy of Charley Harper Art Studio *(top)*. Photo by Ross Van Pelt-RVP Photography.

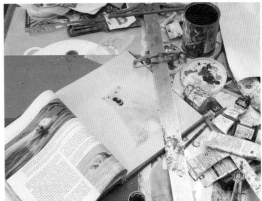

Photo by the author

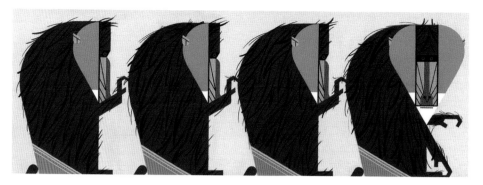

BACKSCRATCHING IN THE BABOONDOCKS

Notice that the biggest baboon is getting his back scratched, but doesn't have to bother with scratching another's back, and the smallest must scratch another's back without getting his scratched in return.
Courtesy of Charley Harper Art Studio. Photo by Ross Van Pelt-RVP Photography

never behave in a way, or be placed in an environment, that was unnatural. Rather than treat animals like humans, Charley chose to make connections between the two, using the basic instincts that both share: protecting our young, seeking food or shelter, feeling amusement, or simply experiencing the joy of having someone scratch an itchy spot we can't reach.

Charley enjoyed coming up with the titles of his pictures as much as he enjoyed painting them. Sometimes the title came first—perhaps in the middle of the night—and sometimes it came later. Either way, Charley felt the title was just as important as the painting itself. And when that title just happened to be a **pun**, Charley was especially excited. He considered puns "the whisks that stir the creative broth . . . leaps of the imagination resulting in the sudden bonding of two previously unconnected and unrelated ideas or words to reveal a new entity —pure, primal creativity."[5]

Charley didn't stop at captions. Usually, each wildlife painting was accompanied by a small essay or commentary. Some of the captions for Charley's earliest bird pictures were written by another writer who contributed to the *Ford Times* magazine, E. B. White. This was not long

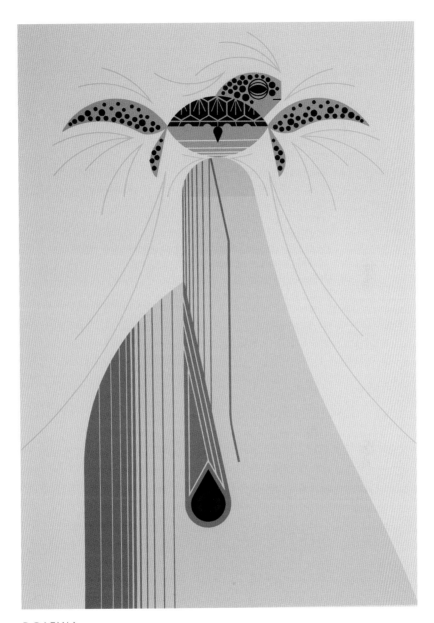

DOLFUN

Charley's captions often contain a pun, or a play on words. This painting of a dolphin having a little fun with a young sea turtle is no exception.
Courtesy of Charley Harper Art Studio. Photo by Ross Van Pelt-RVP Photography

CHARLEY THE WRITER

WHILE CHARLEY HARPER is primarily known for his contribution to the world of art, we also know that Charley had a way with words. The essays accompanying his paintings are filled with humorous puns and are fun to read. Charley wrote more than just the captions to go along with his paintings. *Ford Times* magazine published several articles that were both written and illustrated by Charley.

Charley could turn any outdoor adventure into a great story. A family vacation to West Virginia's Allegheny Mountains became the subject for a magazine article, and a father-son canoe and camping trip along the Daniel Boone Trail became another. Both sported Charley's colorful and unmistakable illustrations. An account of a weeklong sailing trip off the coast of Maine would lead any reader to pick up the phone and make reservations aboard an old-time schooner.

As a writer of letters, Charley was **prolific**, especially during the years he and Edie were separated by the war. His letters often read like short stories, complete with detailed descriptions of colorful characters and sometimes even a bit of suspense.

Charley kept journals off and on throughout his life. Hand-scrawled notes of nature and life can be found throughout his studio, tacked to bulletin boards and tucked into drawers, delightful reminders of his keen sense of observation.

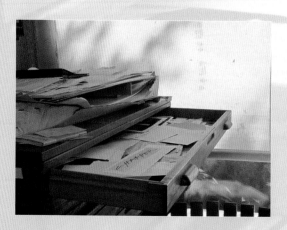

Photo by the author

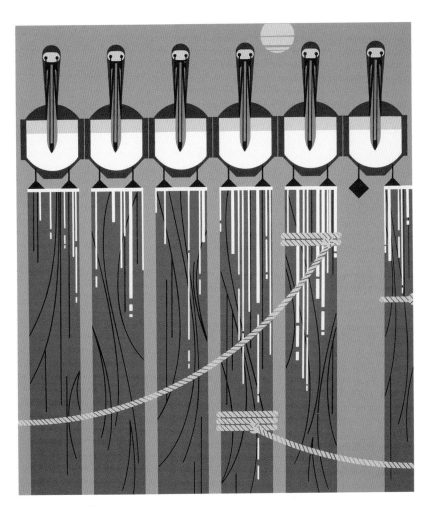

PIER GROUP

The pelicans on the pier feel the need to conform. Some people, like this pelican, will go to great lengths not to stand out.
Courtesy of Charley Harper Art Studio. Photo by Ross Van Pelt-RVP Photography

before White became well known for writing the much-loved children's books *Charlotte's Web* and *Stuart Little*. When White no longer wished to create captions for *Ford Times*, Charley took over. In just a few sentences, Charley was able to convey information about the animal's habitat, often making a connection between the animal's behavior and our own human characteristics.

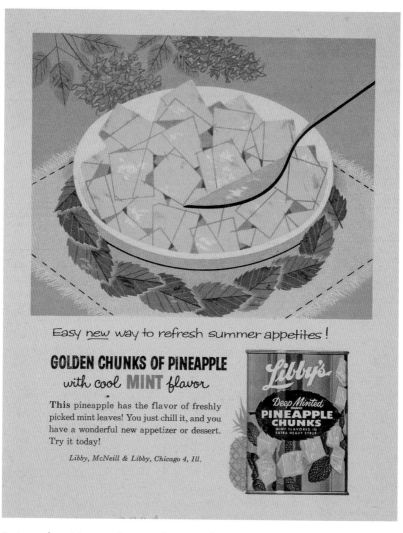

Doing advertising work was a lot more fun once no one was dictating Charley's style.
Courtesy of Charley Harper Art Studio. Photo by Ross Van Pelt-RVP Photography

While Charley continued to illustrate for *Ford Times,* he also created illustrations for a Betty Crocker cookbook (putting his own humorous spin on otherwise dull kitchen scenarios). He did some more commercial art for companies, such as Morton Salt and Sohio (Stan-

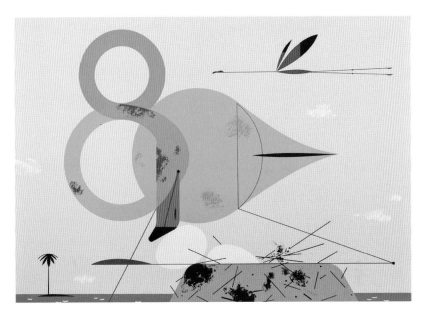

FLAMINGOS

Courtesy of Charley Harper Art Studio. Photo by Ross Van Pelt-RVP Photography

dard Oil of Ohio), but, unlike in his early days working for a commercial art studio, this time he was given the freedom to put his own vision into the work. By now, people were familiar with the Charley Harper style. "They wouldn't ask me to do something unless they liked what they'd seen already,"[6] he explained.

Charley had amassed a large body of work as well as a following of loyal fans. As orders for his popular limited-edition silkscreen prints increased, he partnered with Frame House, a gallery in Louisville, Kentucky. The Frame House Gallery began to market Charley's prints nationally. He also connected with a Cincinnati printer and moved the silkscreening process out of his own studio. That didn't mean he was any less involved. Charley still cut the stencils and then oversaw the difficult process of setting up the colors. The quality of the printing process was very important to Charley, and he was always available to rush to the printer to troubleshoot any problem that would arise.

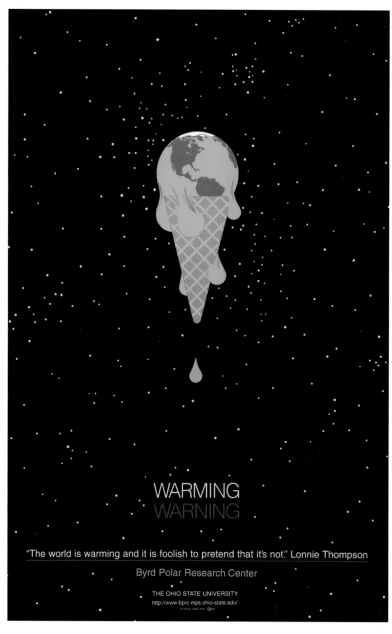

Environmental issues became increasingly important to Charley throughout his life.
Courtesy of Charley Harper Art Studio. Photo by Ross Van Pelt-RVP Photography

He illustrated over fifty biological posters for conservation groups and the National Park Service, including a series of ten national park posters. Because Charley was fully committed to accuracy and detail, he visited each national park, interviewing park rangers and researching the landscape, flora, and fauna.

It was only natural that Charley Harper, the artist and naturalist, would become Charley Harper, the environmentalist. "The more I learn about nature, the more I am troubled by unanswerable questions about human exploitation of plants and animals and our casual assumption that the natural world is here only to serve people,"[7] he said.

Many of his later works depict the damaging impact humans have had on a particular animal's habitat. In 2000, Charley was a guest of the Byrd Polar Research Center at the Ohio State University where he collaborated with researchers and eventually created a painting called *Warming Warning*. It resonated with those who were hoping to bring greater public attention to the possible effects of global warming. *Scary Scenario*, Charley's last painting, was another of his attempts to depict what might happen if the world continued to ignore the signs of climate change—cardinals living with polar bears.

Another role that Charley took on was that of teacher. Naturally, young Brett became his parents' first student and, later, their respected critic. From a very young age, Brett created the family's annual Christmas card, incorporating the ladybug theme into every card. When Charley was doing the illustrations for children's books, it helped to have a young reader in the house to offer an honest opinion.

For some time, Charley returned to the Art Academy of Cincinnati as an instructor. Although he was glad to share his time and talent, he was overly modest regarding his impact on students. Charley was never quite comfortable with his role as teacher and never convinced of his effectiveness. Countless students would prove him wrong, later expressing their deep appreciation for his teaching and wisdom.

Charley Harper was humble, both in art and in life. He made every painting look so simple, so easy, that an observer might never appreciate the hours spent planning, researching, sketching, drawing, and painting.

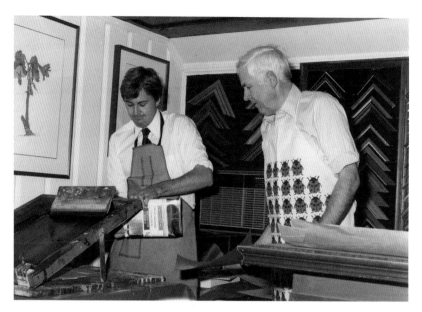

Charley and Brett spent a lot of time together, both inside and outside of the art studio.
Courtesy of Charley Harper Art Studio. Photo by Edie Harper

Did an accomplished artist like Charley ever have doubts? Charley explained it like this:

> Each new painting is so difficult to birth that each one makes me feel as if I have never painted before. Whatever the reason, each picture brings a period of total depression, utter discouragement, frustration, hopelessness. (I can't do it, I'll never be able to paint another picture, whatever made me think I could be an artist?) Then, it begins to take shape, everything falls into place and there comes a feeling of ecstasy, of rightness, certainty: *of course,* this is the way it had to be, why did it take me so long to unlock the secret?[8]

Art fans and nature lovers alike are awfully glad Charley stuck with it long enough to unlock thousands of secrets.

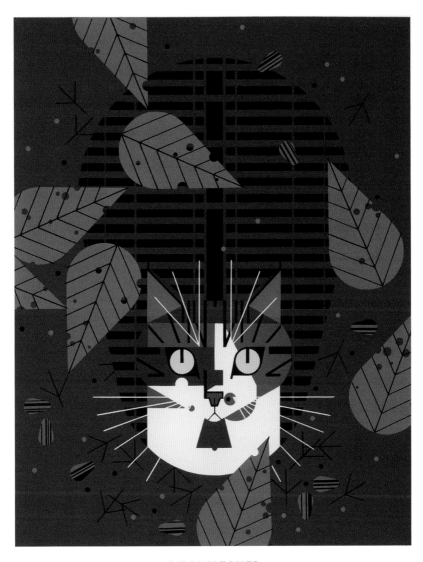

BIRDWATCHER

Courtesy of Charley Harper Art Studio.
Photo by Ross Van Pelt-RVP Photography

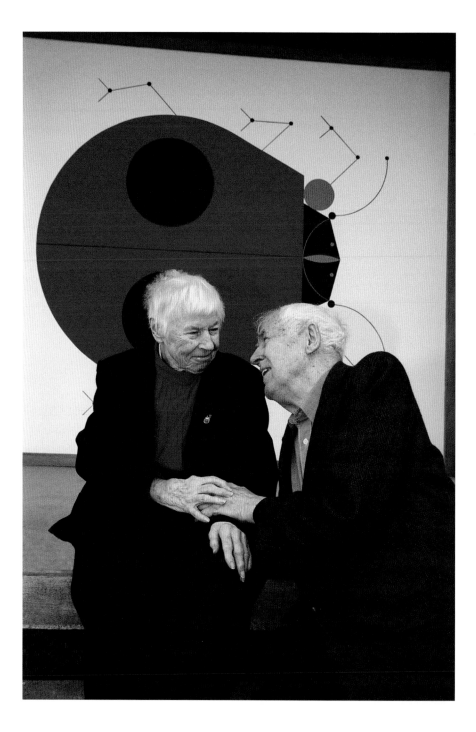

8

FINISHING WELL

I've never seen any other imagery that appeals to grannies and hipsters alike.

—Todd Oldham, fashion designer[1]

W ITH EDIE AND a tiger cat named Gussie by his side, Charley grew old in his Cincinnati home and studio.

The passing of time ages everyone, but some things never get old, and Charley's art has proven to have lasting appeal. Charley's first fans were most likely the readers of *Ford Times* magazine in the 1950s and 1960s. His youngest at the time were probably readers of *The Giant Golden Book of Biology* or the *Childcraft Encyclopedia*.

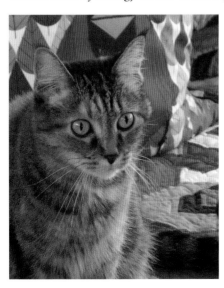

Charley and Edie were married nearly sixty years. They spent almost fifty years together in the home they built in Cincinnati. Gussie, the housecat, still resides at the Harpers' home.
Courtesy of Charley Harper Art Studio. Photo by Gordon Baer *(opposite page)*. Photo by the author *(left)*

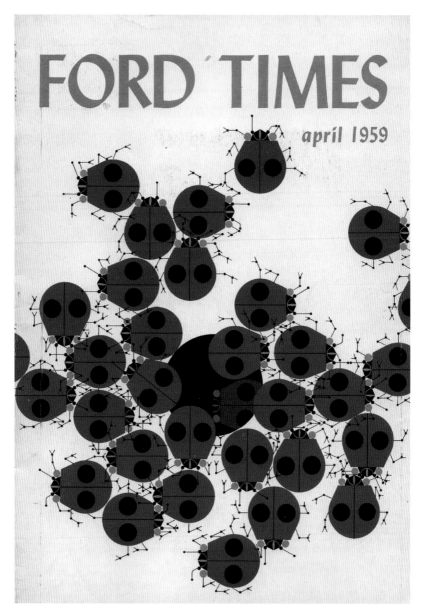

FORD TIMES

april 1959

If the cardinal was Charley's signature symbol, the ladybug came to personify the Harper family and home.

Used with permission from Ford Images

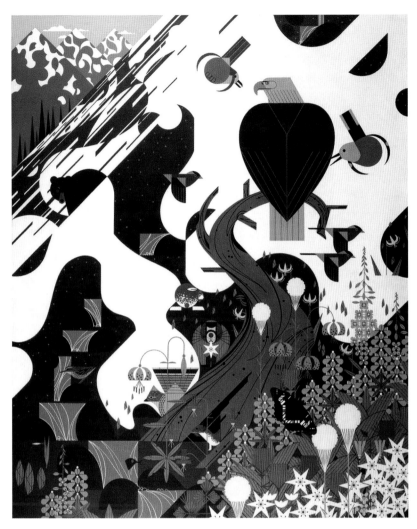

Charley was commissioned to create posters for ten national parks. He visited each one, including the Alpine Northwest, pictured here.
Courtesy of Charley Harper Art Studio. Photo by Ross Van Pelt-RVP Photography

Anyone traveling in the 1970s was sure to come across his work on park posters and Delta Airlines posters.

His wildlife prints had caught the attention of art collectors and nature lovers in the 1970s and beyond. Charley was featured in *Ranger Rick*, the magazine for children from the National Wildlife Federation.

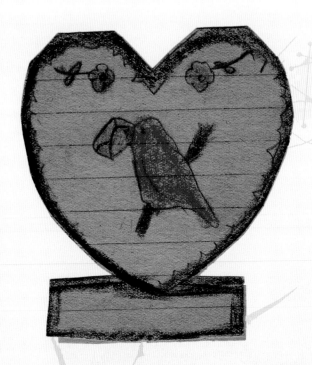

THE HARPER CARDINAL EVOLVES

FOR MANY YEARS, Charley believed that the first cardinal he drew was for a 1954 issue of *Ford Times* magazine *(facing page, top)*. But Harper archivist Chip Doyle recently discovered that Charley must have had birds on the brain much earlier. A Valentine card from young Charley to his sister Ruth sports a cardinal in crayon *(above)*. Eventually, Charley decided that he preferred a straight-on view of the bright red bird *(facing page, bottom)*. That is the cardinal that became a Harper trademark.

Courtesy of Charley Harper Art Studio.
Photo by Ross Van Pelt-RVP Photography

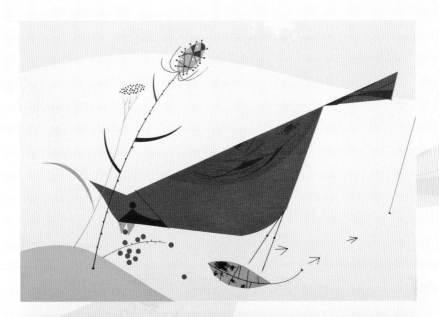

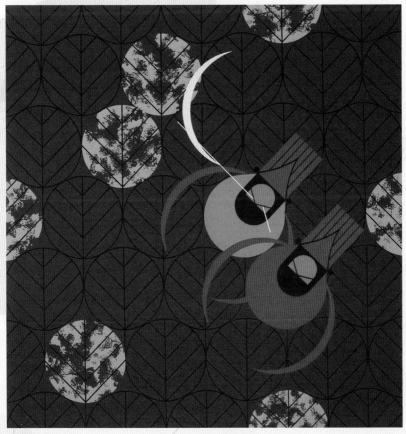

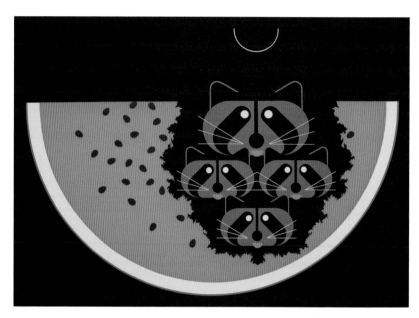

WATERMELON MOON

Courtesy of Charley Harper Art Studio. Photo by Ross Van Pelt-RVP Photography

It was a successful art career, spanning six decades. Charley had been able to make a living doing something he loved. Not everyone can say that.

All of this would have been enough—it would have been more than enough—for a humble fellow like Charley, but there was more to come. A new generation of wildlife enthusiasts and art fans would fall in love with Charley Harper, and much of the credit would go to celebrity New York designer Todd Oldham, who "rediscovered" Charley's work in 2002.

Todd was a child in the 1960s when he first discovered *The Giant Golden Book of Biology* among a stack of books at school in Texas. At the time, he paid no attention to who had drawn the cells, plants, and animals, but he knew they were fascinating to look at. Charley's art brought science to life for Todd, and those images stuck with him for years.

Many years later, the successful fashion designer was browsing around an antique store in Pennsylvania and stumbled upon a pile of old *Ford Times* magazines. When he saw Charley's birds on the covers, he was immediately drawn to them, but it would be a year before he made the connection between his newfound affinity for the *Ford Times* artist and his childhood fascination with *The Giant Golden Book of Biology*. Once he figured it out, he had to meet Charley Harper.

It didn't take long for these two creative souls—the artist and the designer—to become friends, and soon after, Charley's art was appearing on sofas and chairs Oldham designed for La-Z-Boy furniture. Later, T-shirts at Old Navy stores were sporting Charley's easily recognizable creatures as well. Eventually, Todd and his studio associates in New York compiled Charley's art into a book titled *Charley Harper: An Illustrated Life*. Now, a person can drink from a Harper mug, and young children can fall asleep on a tiger pillow under a comforter covered with Harper animals.

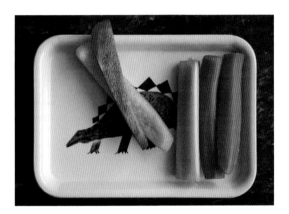
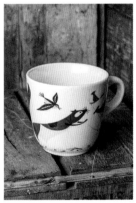
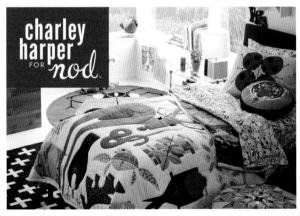

Charley's collaboration with well-known New York designer Todd Oldham has led the way to, among others, a dinnerware line from Fishs Eddy (*top*), and a selection of children's décor from The Land of Nod.
Courtesy of Fishs Eddy, LLC and The Land of Nod

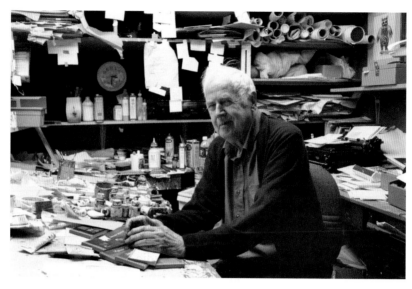

Charley at work in his studio.
Courtesy of Charley Harper Art Studio. Photo by Sam Cauffield

The friendship between Todd and Charley resulted in a 2006 exhibit at Cincinnati's Contemporary Arts Center. Titled *Graphic Content: Contemporary and Modern/Art and Design,* the exhibition was **curated** by Matt Distel, with Todd Oldham overseeing design graphics and installation. Highlighted were midcentury modern artists, including Charley and Edie, along with four other esteemed masters. Charley had never expected to have his work on display at the Contemporary Arts Center, where usually only the most innovative work of the day is shown. Charley's work had withstood the test of time.

"I don't how to express my thanks to you for making this last chapter in my life the most interesting,"[2] a grateful Charley told Todd during a radio interview in December 2006. Todd responded with similar gratitude, saying, "I really feel like I'm doing a public service, because the more people that get to be in contact with your art, the richer the world becomes."[3]

Six months later, Charley passed away at the age of eighty-four.

Todd Oldham once asked Charley Harper what brought him more joy: seeing his works in print or the process of painting them? Charley answered thoughtfully:

> I think finally finishing a painting and getting it to satisfy me is the high point. And seeing it reproduced somewhere is fine, too, but just finishing painting it—that's the best part.[4]

DID YOU KNOW?

Charley Harper's amazingly bold graphics translated to the skateboarding scene in 2008 when Habitat Skateboards teamed up with Charley Harper Art Studio. *On the Prowl, Poison Dart Frog, Anaconda and Jaguar,* **and** *Serengeti Spaghetti* **are just a few of Charley's paintings that became popular skateboard decks.**

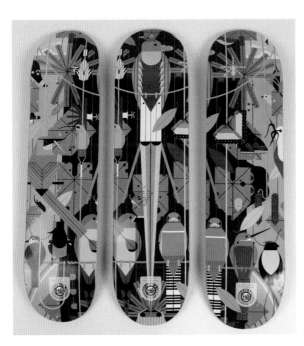

Charley Harper's colorful images lend themselves to some excellent skateboard designs.
Harper x Habitat collection, 2010. Skate decks borrowed from the Donovan family

9

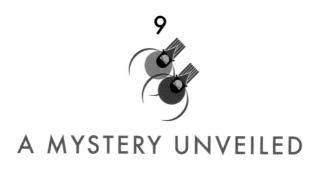

A MYSTERY UNVEILED

It's not often you're given the opportunity to see something for the first time—again.

—from the video, *Charley Harper "Space Walk" Mural Unveiling*[1]

O N A TUESDAY afternoon in November 2015, a large crowd gathered inside the Duke Energy Convention Center in downtown Cincinnati, Ohio. Everyone was there for the same reason—to find out just what had been hidden beneath a layer of drywall for nearly three decades.

Charley's son, Brett, and New York designer and family friend, Todd Oldham, had the honor of unveiling *Space Walk*, a set of two ceramic tile murals designed by Charley Harper in 1970. The abstract designs, inspired by Neil Armstrong's walk on the moon, are special because only a few of Charley's tile murals can be seen on public display, and because these are the only abstract murals he ever created. Each mural is thirty-five feet long and twelve feet high and each is made up of 60,480 one-inch ceramic tiles. Because abstract art is not an exact representation of its subject, *Space Walk* fascinates onlookers. Some see spacecraft; others see tumbling astronauts.

But the question remained: Why were these two murals concealed in the first place?

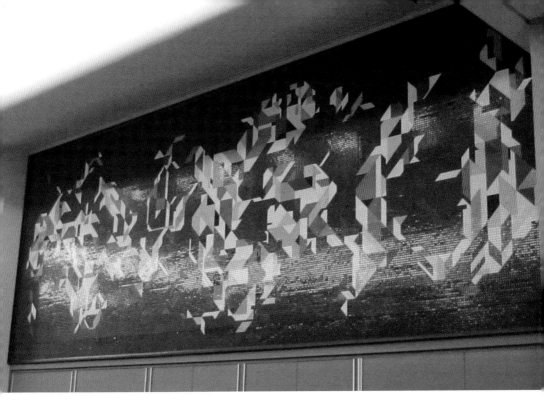

SPACE WALK

After restoration, one half of *Space Walk* can be seen over each of the two main entrances to the exhibit hall at the Duke Energy Convention Center in downtown Cincinnati, Ohio.
Photo by the author

In 1987, seventeen years after the murals were installed, the convention center underwent a major renovation, and it was determined that the murals no longer fit the décor. That choice soon proved to be an unfortunate one—one that has caused a little embarrassment to the decision-makers. In 2002, Charley's collaboration with Todd Oldham brought his artwork once more to the forefront. The Harpers' inclusion in the Contemporary Art Center's 2006 exhibit, *Graphic Content,* further secured Charley's place as a local celebrity, and a 2011–12 exhibit in Hamburg, Germany, added to his international recognition. By 2013, a Cincinnati group dedicated to the promotion and preservation of modern art began pushing the city council to uncover the hidden murals.

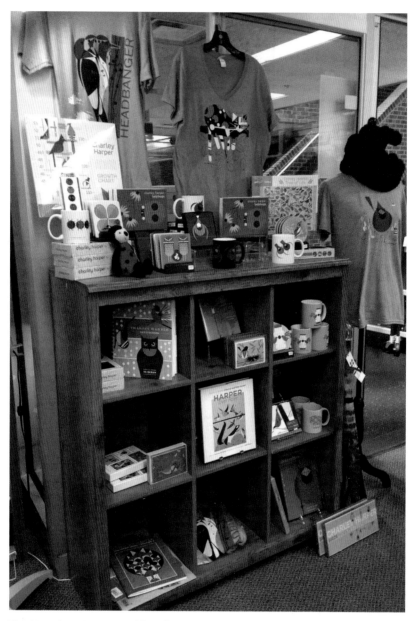

The Hamilton County Public Library in downtown Cincinnati, Ohio, offers a variety of popular items featuring Charley Harper designs.
Photo by the author

Fortunately, instead of removing or destroying the artwork in the 1987 renovations, the murals were merely covered, encased in a drywall tomb, where they would remain hidden for twenty-eight years. In 2014, test holes were cut in the walls to determine the exact location and condition of the murals. Artists from a local tile maker, Koverman Mosaic, were called in to repair and restore the damaged lower sections of each mural. Though it was a challenge, the Kovermans were able to make tiles to match the exact color and sheen of the tiles Charley had selected forty-four years earlier.

Finally, as businessmen, art enthusiasts, and local politicians watched, *Space Walk* came back to life. Although Charley wasn't there to see it, his son Brett was certain his father "would have been moved to tears to see his mural see the light of day once more."[2]

These days, Charley Harper's art can be found almost everywhere. While giant murals grace multistory buildings, smaller versions of his work adorn notecards, calendars, T-shirts, housewares, fabric, puzzles, and umbrellas. There is even a new line of baby and children's accessories, assuring a new generation of fans who'll grow up dazzled by bright red cardinals, cheeky raccoons, and the man who created them.

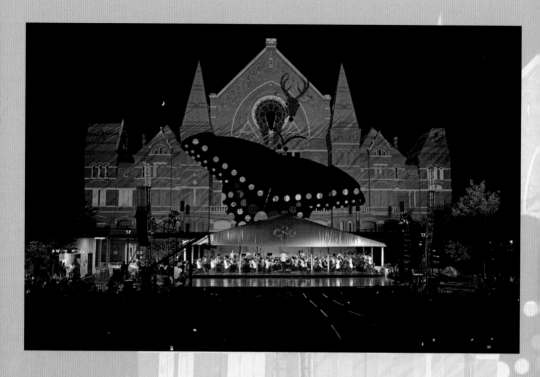

During the summer of 2014, Charley Harper's art was projected in a larger-than-life format on the exterior of Cincinnati's Music Hall.
Courtesy of the Cincinnati Symphony Orchestra

LUMENOCITY 2014

IN AUGUST 2014, Cincinnati honored Charley Harper in a big way—a really, really big way.

The Cincinnati Symphony Orchestra offered a free outdoor concert in Washington Park at the center of the city's Over-the-Rhine neighborhood. The backdrop of the concert was Cincinnati's beautiful Music Hall, and the building itself was the canvas for an amazing lightshow. For three consecutive nights, Charley Harper's birds soared, his frogs leapt, and his fish dove in spectacular color before an audience of thousands.

It was a tribute Charley would never have imagined receiving. And, when the orchestra's first notes rang out, what songfilled the summer night? It was, fittingly, Aaron Copland's *Fanfare for the Common Man.* Humble Charley would have been pleased.

If you chuckle when you look at one of my wildlife prints, I'll be happy. And if you tell me, "Hey, that's right, but I never thought of it that way," I'll be delighted. I like to believe I'm showing you an alternative way of looking at nature.[3]

—Charley Harper

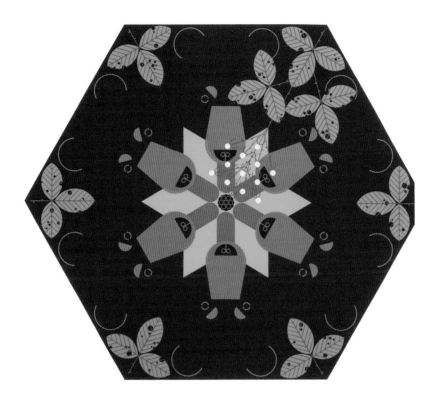

BLACKBEARY JAM

Courtesy of Charley Harper Art Studio.
Photo by Ross Van Pelt-RVP Photography

Charley's Timeline

August 4, 1922

Charles Harper is born near French Creek, West Virginia.

June 1939

Charley graduates from Buckhannon Upshur High School.

September 1939–May 1940

Charley attends West Virginia Wesleyan College in Buckhannon.

September 1940

Charley arrives by train in Cincinnati, Ohio, to attend the Art Academy of Cincinnati. He meets Edith McKee on the first day of class.

September 1940–November 1942

Charley studies at the Art Academy of Cincinnati.

December 9, 1942

Charley enlists in the United States Army.

December 1942–September 1944

Charley trains as a soldier in U.S. military camps in Arkansas, Delaware, and Colorado.

September 7, 1944

Charley and the 414th Infantry Regiment land in Cherbourg, France.

July 2, 1945

The SS *John Ericsson* leaves France bound for the U.S. with Charley on board.

November 6, 1945

Charley is discharged from the United States Army.

January 10, 1946

Charley arrives in New York City to study art at the Art Students League of New York.

September 1946

Charley returns to study at the Art Academy of Cincinnati.

August 1947

Charley graduates from the Art Academy of Cincinnati and wins the first Stephen H. Wilder Traveling Scholarship Award.

August 9, 1947

Charley Harper and Edith McKee are married.

1947

Charley and Edie travel the United States together on a working honeymoon.

1948

Charley begins work at C. H. Schaten Art Studio.

Charley creates his first illustrations for *Ford Times* magazine.

1951

Charley creates his first cover for *Ford Times* magazine.

Charley is hired to create a Model T mural for the Ford Rotunda in Dearborn, Michigan. The building, including Charley's mural, was destroyed by fire in 1962.

May 29, 1953

Brett Harper, the only child of Charley and Edie Harper, is born.

1958

The Harpers build a new home and studio in Finneytown.

Betty Crocker's Dinner for Two is published.

1961

The Giant Golden Book of Biology is published.

1964

Charley creates *Space for all Species*, a mosaic mural in the John Weld Peck Federal Building in Cincinnati, Ohio.

1968

The Animal Kingdom is published.

1970

The *Space Walk* mosaic mural is installed in the Cincinnati Convention Exposition Center (renamed the Duke Energy Convention Center in 2006).

1974

Charley is awarded an Honorary Doctorate of Humane Letters degree from West Virginia Wesleyan College.

1986

The *Web of Life* mosaic mural is installed at Miami University's Pearson Hall.

1987

The *Space Walk* mosaic mural is covered during convention center renovations.

1994

Beguiled by the Wild is published.

December 2006–February 2007

Charley's art is featured in part 1 of the exhibit, *Graphic Content: Contemporary and Modern/Art and Design,* at the Contemporary Arts Center, Cincinnati, Ohio.

2007

Charley and Edie Harper's early works appear together in the exhibit *Minimal Realism* at the Cincinnati Art Museum, Cincinnati, Ohio.

June 10, 2007

Charley Harper passes away in Ohio.

2013

Harper Ever After, an exhibit of Charley and Edie's work, is held at the Art Academy of Cincinnati.

November 10, 2015

The *Space Walk* mosaic mural restoration is revealed at the Duke Energy Convention Center in Cincinnati, Ohio.

2007—present

Charley Harper's work continues to be exhibited worldwide. His art is shown within the U.S. in several states, including California, Texas, and Washington; and in a number of European cities, including Hamburg and Berlin, Germany, and London, England.

Glossary

abstract: in fine art, a work that emphasizes line and color, representing the idea of an object

Allied soldiers: the group of forces united against the Axis Powers (Italy, Japan, and other allies of Nazi Germany) in World War II

anthropomorphism: the act of assigning human behaviors or characteristics to an animal

archivist: a person who preserves or organizes a collection of materials

art director: the person responsible for the selection and design of art for a book or magazine

bayonet: a sharp point or blade attached to the end of a gun and used in hand-to-hand combat

beachcombers: people who spend their time on the beach collecting items that have washed ashore

censored: written or spoken words that have been reviewed and/or had parts removed that were determined unacceptable for a given situation

civilians: nonmilitary personnel

commander in chief: another name for the president, one that describes his role as the head of the armed forces

commercial artist: an artist who creates illustrations and graphics for advertising

compass: a hinged tool used for drawing perfect circles

conservationist: a person who acts to preserve the natural world

correspondence course: a class where instruction is provided and feedback is given by mail

curate: in an exhibit, the act of choosing works and acquiring works of art

curator: the person responsible for selecting pieces for an art collection

cyst: a thin-walled membraneous sac or cavity containing fluid

darkroom: a room or space from which normal light is excluded for the purpose of handling and developing film

draft: the means by which military forces can require service

film processing: the printing of photographs taken by a traditional camera

foxhole: a small hole, dug to provide shelter for a soldier during battle

freelance: work in which a person is not hired continuously, but on a project-by-project basis

French curve: a drawing tool for making curved lines

galleries: buildings or rooms where artists display or sell their work

Gerridae: a family of insects commonly known as water striders, water bugs, pond skaters, water skippers, or Jesus bugs. Classified as true bugs, they distinguish themselves by having the unique ability to walk on water.

GI: from the phrase "government-issued," commonly used to describe a person who is or was enlisted in the armed forces

infantry division: a large group of soldiers, usually numbering between 10,000 and 30,000, often broken up into several regiments

infantry regiment: a group of soldiers, usually numbering between 2,000 and 4,000, that serves as a unit of a division

intelligence: in war, gathering information about an enemy, such as their location, intentions, numbers, or supplies

KP: a term meaning "kitchen duty" that has been defined as both "kitchen police" and "kitchen patrol"

la mer: in French, the sea

liberators: those who set others free from the control of an oppressive government

memorabilia: items connected with special or unusual events

minimal realism: the phrase Charley Harper created to describe his art style—realistic but with the least amount of detail possible

mosaic: a picture or pattern created of many small pieces of glass, stone, or tile laid together

monotonous: boring or unchanging

multiple sclerosis: a serious disease of the nervous system that worsens over time, gradually causing permanent loss of movement and or/senses

nibs: the metal writing tips of an ink pen

prolific: producing something in large quantities, such as writings or works of art

pun: the use of multiple meanings or similar-sounding words or phrases in such a way as to create a humorous result

reconnaissance: exploring and observing an area to gain information during war

serigraphy/silkscreening: a process for making prints in which a stencil permits color to pass through a fine mesh onto paper

spring peepers: the nickname for a tree frog found in the eastern United States, whose loud, shrill call is common in the early spring

stateside: in the continental United States

strike: a tactic used by organized workers who stop working for a period of time in order to make a case for better wages or working conditions

T-square: a drawing tool useful in making right angles

terrain: the physical characteristics of an area of land

worry wart: a person who fusses needlessly over something

Acknowledgments

My trip to the Charley Harper Art Studio described earlier in this book was the first of many. This book would have never been written without the enthusiastic cooperation of Brett Harper and the tireless and forgiving assistance of Chip Doyle, who could find anything in an amazingly brief period of time.

I am grateful to Brett for his willingness to share hundreds of pages of family artifacts including letters, essays, scrapbooks, and photographs.

The historians and archivists at the Art Academy of Cincinnati, West Virginia Wesleyan College, and the Upshur County Historical Society provided support at just the right times.

Finally, I'm grateful to Gillian Berchowitz, whose vision for this biography series was clear long before it began, and whose out-loud thought, "What about Charley Harper?" sent me on one of the most rewarding research and writing adventures of my career.

Notes

Chapter One: A Mural Mystery

1. Steven Rosen, "Charley Harper's 'Space Walk' mural is unveiled at the Convention Center after being hidden for decades," *Citybeat,* November 4, 2015, http://www.citybeat.com/arts-culture/visual-arts/article/13001366/lost-and-found.

Chapter Two: An Artist Is Born

1. *The Art of Charley Harper: A Retrospective View,* DVD, Dan Hadley Productions, 2005.

2. Todd Oldham, *Charley Harper: An Illustrated Life* (Los Angeles: AMMO Books, 2009), 16.

3. *The Art of Charley Harper: A Retrospective View.*

4. Oldham, *Charley Harper: An Illustrated Life,* 17.

5. Charley Harper to Edith McKee, letter, November 26, 1942, Charley Harper Art Studio.

6. Brett Harper, interview, October 16, 2015.

7. Charley Harper to Edith McKee, letter, June 30, 1941, Charley Harper Art Studio.

8. Charley Harper to Edith McKee, letter, November 23, 1942, Charley Harper Art Studio.

9. Todd Wilkinson, "Illusions in Simplicity," *Wildlife Art News,* November–December 1992, 50.

10. National Wildlife Federation, "Water Strider," http://www.nwf.org/wildlife/wildlife-library/invertebrates/water-strider.aspx.

Chapter Three: The Artist Becomes a Soldier

1. Charley Harper to Edith McKee, letter, November 26, 1942.

2. Ibid.

3. Charley Harper to Edith McKee, letter, November 25, 1942, Charley Harper Art Studio.

4. Charley Harper to Edith McKee, letter, December 23, 1942, Charley Harper Art Studio.

5. Charley Harper to Edith McKee, letter, December 24, 1942, Charley Harper Art Studio.

6. Charley Harper to Edith McKee, letter, December 25, 1942, Charley Harper Art Studio.

7. Ibid.

8. Charley Harper to Edith McKee, letter, January 14, 1943, Charley Harper Art Studio.

9. Charley Harper to Edith McKee, letter, May 27, 1943, Charley Harper Art Studio.

Chapter Four: The Soldier Goes to War

1. Charley Harper to Edith McKee, letter, October 20, 1944, Charley Harper Art Studio.

2. Charley Harper to Edith McKee, letter, March 10, 1944, Charley Harper Art Studio.

3. Ibid.

4. Charley Harper to Edith McKee, letter, April 4, 1944, Charley Harper Art Studio.

5. Charley Harper to Edith McKee, letter, October 22, 1944, Charley Harper Art Studio.

6. Charley Harper to Edith McKee, letter, March 26, 1945, Charley Harper Art Studio.

7. Charley Harper to Edith McKee, letter, May 7, 1945, Charley Harper Art Studio.

8. Charley Harper to Edith McKee, letter, October 3, 1945, Charley Harper Art Studio.

9. Charley Harper to Edith McKee, letter, November 6, 1945, Charley Harper Art Studio.

10. Smithsonian National Postal Museum, "Victory Mail Online Exhibit," http://postalmuseum.si.edu/victorymail/index.html.

Chapter Five: A Country Boy in the Big City

1. Charley Harper to Edith McKee, letter, January 10, 1946, Charley Harper Art Studio.

2. Charley Harper, print folder content, Frame House Gallery, 1969, Charley Harper Art Studio.

3. Charley Harper to Edith McKee, letter, January 8, 1946, Charley Harper Art Studio.

4. Charley Harper to Edith McKee, letter, January 10, 1946.

5. Charley Harper to Edith McKee, letter, January 11, 1946, Charley Harper Art Studio.

6. Charley Harper to Edith McKee, letter, January 16, 1946, Charley Harper Art Studio.

7. Charley Harper to Edith McKee, letter, January 17, 1946, Charley Harper Art Studio.

8. Charley Harper to Edith McKee, letter, January 24, 1946, Charley Harper Art Studio.

9. Ibid.

10. Charley Harper to Edith McKee, letter, January 15, 1946, Charley Harper Art Studio.

11. Charley Harper to Edith McKee, letter, February 28, 1946, Charley Harper Art Studio.

12. Charley Harper to Edith McKee, letter, January 25, 1946, Charley Harper Art Studio.

13. Charley Harper to Edith McKee, letter, March 18, 1946, Charley Harper Art Studio.

14. Charley Harper to Edith McKee, letter, March 20, 1946, Charley Harper Art Studio.

15. Charley Harper to Edith McKee, letter, February 15, 1946, Charley Harper Art Studio.

16. Ibid.

17. Charley Harper to Edith McKee, letter, June 6, 1946, Charley Harper Art Studio.

Chapter Six: Finding That Charley Harper Style

1. Todd Wilkinson, "Illusions in Simplicity," 46.

2. *The Art of Charley Harper: A Retrospective View.*

3. Edith Harper to Marjorie Keil, letter, September 30, 1947, Charley Harper Art Studio.

4. Ibid.

5. Jessica Flores Garcia, "Go Fish: The Dish on Charley Harper," *Modernism*, Winter 2011–12, 54.

6. Charley Harper to Mr. Wood Hannah Sr., undated letter, http://www
.charleyharperprints.com/charley-harper/his-story-in-his-own-words.

7. Ibid.

8. Charley Harper and Roger Caras, *Beguiled by the Wild* (Gaithersburg,
MD: Flower Valley Press, 1994), 7.

9. Charley Harper, "Charles Harper, Minimal Realist," undated essay,
Charley Harper Art Studio.

10. *The Art of Charley Harper: A Retrospective View.*

11. Charley Harper, "Artist's Questionnaire," undated essay, Charley Harper
Art Studio.

12. *The Art of Charley Harper: A Retrospective View.*

13. Oldham, *Charley Harper: An Illustrated Life,* 29.

14. Jane Yolen, "Fly a Kite with the Champion," cover and text illustrations by Charles Harper, *Ford Times,* March 1962, 2–6.

Chapter Seven: Wild about Charley

1. Andrea to Charley Harper, undated letter, Charley Harper Art Studio.

2. Harper, "Charles Harper, Minimal Realist."

3. Charley Harper to Mr. Wood Hannah Sr., undated letter.

4. Oldham, *Charley Harper: An Illustrated Life,* 24.

5. Charley Harper and Roger Caras, *Beguiled by the Wild,* 9.

6. Oldham, *Charley Harper: An Illustrated Life,* 29.

7. Charley Harper, Frame House Gallery interview, 1974, Charley Harper
Art Studio.

8. Charley Harper, "Artist's Questionnaire."

Chapter Eight: Finishing Well

1. Liz Logan, "Wild about Charley Harper's Nature Art," *Wall Street Journal,*
September 24, 2015, http://www.wsj.com/articles/wild-about-charley-harpers
-nature-art-1443103780.

2. *Todd Oldham's Interview with Charley Harper,* WVXU 91.7 radio, December 2006, http://www.youtube.com/watch?v=u-MVyfu7anY.

3. Ibid.

4. Oldham, *Charley Harper: An Illustrated Life,* 44.

Chapter Nine: A Mystery Unveiled

1. Linda Jensen and Jason Snell, *Charley Harper* Space Walk *Mural Unveiling*, Duke Energy Convention Center, December 2015, http://www.youtube.com/watch?v=H1hBJspo5rc.

2. Sharon Coolidge, "Convention Center re-do to reveal hidden Harper mural," *Cincinnati,* August 13, 2014, http://www.cincinnati.com/story/news/politics/2014/08/13/convention-center-re-reveal-hidden-harper-mural/13964771/.

3. Charley Harper, miscellaneous documents, Charley Harper Art Studio.

Bibliography

Books

Ames, Gerald, and Rose Wyler. *The Giant Golden Book of Biology: An Introduction to the Science of Life.* Illustrated by Charles Harper. New York: Golden Press, 1961.

Caswell-Pearce, Sara, and Brett Harper. *Harper Ever After: The Early Work of Charley and Edie Harper.* Illustrated by Charley and Edie Harper. Portland, OR: Pomegranate, 2015.

Crocker, Betty. *Betty Crocker's Dinner for Two: Cook Book.* Illustrated by Charles Harper. New York: Golden Press, 1958.

Harper, Charley, and Roger Caras. *Beguiled by the Wild: The Art of Charley Harper.* Gaithersburg, MD: Flower Valley Press, 1994.

Hoegh, Leo Arthur, and Howard J. Doyle, editors. *Timberwolf Tracks: 104th Infantry Division.* Washington: Infantry Journal Press, 1946. Reprinted as *Timberwolf Tracks: The History of the 104th Infantry Division, 1942–1945.* Whitefish, MT: Literary Licensing, LLC, 2012.

Oldham, Todd. *Charley Harper: An Illustrated Life.* Los Angeles: AMMO Books, 2009.

Untermeyer, Bryna, and Louis Untermeyer, editors. *Creatures Wild and Tame: The Golden Treasury of Children's Literature, Vol. 7.* Illustrated by Charles Harper. New York: Golden Press, 1963.

Articles

Churchman, Deborah. "Ladybug Love." *Ranger Rick*, November–December 1996, 4–10.

Coolidge, Sharon. "Convention Center Re-do to Reveal Hidden Harper Mural." *Cincinnati,* August 13, 2014. http://www.cincinnati.com/story/news/politics/2014/08/13/convention-center-re-reveal-hidden-harper-mural/13964771.

Doane, Kathleen. "Charley Harper and Todd Oldham." *Cincinnati Magazine*, December 2006, 160–233.

Feagler, Linda. "Animal Kingdom." *Ohio Magazine,* August 2016, 12–15.

Garcia, Jessica Flores. "Go Fish: The Dish on Charley Harper." *Modernism,* Winter 2011–12, 52–58.

Gelfand, Janelle. "Harper Ever After: A Time Capsule of Art and Love." The *Cincinnati Enquirer,* March 22, 2015, 6D–7D.

Harper, Charles. "Canoeing on the Cumberland." Cover and interior illustrations by Charles Harper. *Ford Times,* May 1968, 30–36.

———. "Low Gear on the High Road." Cover and interior illustrations by Charles Harper. *Ford Times,* July 1962, 22–24.

———. "Two Weeks before the Mast." Interior illustration by Charles Harper. *Ford Times,* May 1963, 40–43.

———. "West Virginia's Vertical Vacationland." Cover and interior illustrations by Charles Harper. *Ford Times,* June 1963, 28–31.

Hughes, Jim. "A Charley Harper Retrospective." http://www.codex99.com /illustration/133.html, 2013–2015.

Kieffer, Nina. "Home is where the art is." *Hometrends,* March 2011, 29–32.

Logan, Liz. "Wild about Charley Harper's Nature Art." *Wall Street Journal,* September 24, 2015. http://www.wsj.com/articles/wild-about-charley-harpers -nature-art-1443103780.

National Wildlife Federation. "Water Strider." http://www.nwf.org/wildlife/ wildlife-library/invertebrates/water-strider.aspx.

Rosen, Stephen. "Charley Harper's 'Space Walk' Mural Is Unveiled at the Convention Center after Being Hidden for Decades." *Citybeat,* November 4, 2015. http://www.citybeat.com/arts-culture/visual-arts/article/13001366 /lost-and-found.

Wilkinson, Todd. "Illusions in Simplicity." *Wildlife Art News,* November– December 1992, 46–51.

Yolen, Jane. "Fly a Kite with the Champion." Cover and interior illustrations by Charles Harper. *Ford Times,* March 1962, 2–6.

Interviews

Doyle, Chip. Cincinnati, Ohio. October 30, 2015, November 23, 2015, and September 16, 2016.

Harper, Brett. Telephone interview. June 2, 2015.

Harper, Brett. Cincinnati, Ohio. October 16 and 30, 2015, and September 16, 2016.

Jensen, Linda. Cincinnati, Ohio. February 26, 2016.

Koverman, Marcia. Telephone interview. July 7, 2016.

Video Recordings

At Home with Charley Harper. Designtex. Birdling Films with Todd Oldham, 2007.

The Art of Charley Harper: A Retrospective View. DVD. Dan Hadley Productions, 2005.

Frame House Gallery interview with Charley Harper, 1974. http://www.charleyharper.com/about-charley/faq.html.

Jensen, Linda, and Jason Snell. *Charley Harper* Space Walk *Mural Unveiling*. Duke Energy Convention Center, December 2015. http://www.youtube.com/watch?v=H1hBJspo5rc.

Todd Oldham's Interview with Charley Harper. WVXU 91.7 radio, December 2006. http://www.youtube.com/watch?v=u-MVyfu7anY.

Untitled video presentation. April 13, 1991. Charley Harper Art Studio.

Miscellaneous Writings

Doyle, Chip. *Charley Harper: A Bird's Eye View*. Exhibit catalog. University of Cincinnati, Reed Gallery, January 12–February 16, 2012.

Harper, Brett. "The Silkscreen Art of Charles Harper." Undated essay. Charley Harper Art Studio.

Harper, Charles. "Artist's Questionnaire." Undated essay. Charley Harper Art Studio.

———. "Beauty and Function." Undated essay. Charley Harper Art Studio.

———. "Charles Harper, Minimal Realist." Undated essay. Charley Harper Art Studio.

———. Letters to Edith McKee. 1941–1946. Charley Harper Art Studio.

———. Letter to Marjorie Keil. August 28, 1947. Charley Harper Art Studio.

———. Letter to Mr. Wood Hannah Sr. 1967. http://www.charleyharperprints.com/charley-harper/his-story-in-his-own-words.

———. Print folder content. Frame House Gallery. 1969. Charley Harper Art Studio.

Harper, Edith. Letter to Marjorie Keil. September 30, 1947. Charley Harper Art Studio.

Resume. Charley Harper Art Studio. http://www.charleyharperartstudio.com/shop/Resume.

Smithsonian National Postal Museum. "Victory Mail Online Exhibit." http://postalmuseum.si.edu/victorymail/index.html.

Biographies for Young Readers

Michelle Houts, Series Editor